Other Books by R

What Managers Need

Productivity and Results

Performance Based Management

Rate Yourself as a Manager

You're in Charge: A Guide for Business and Personal Success

The Inside Advantage

Nobody Gets Rich Working for Somebody Else

Personal Performance Contracts

*If They Can—You Can! Lessons from America's
New Breed of Successful Entrepreneurs*

Rate Your Executive Potential

Management Ideas That Work

How to Export: Everything You Need to Know to Get Started

Ready, Aim, HIRE! (Co-author)

*The Entrepreneurial Family: How to Sustain
the Vision and Value in Your Family Business*

*Family Ties and Business Binds: How to Solve
the Inevitable Problems of Family Businesses*

Think Like a Manager

Sleep Disorders: America's Hidden Nightmare

*Sales Manager's High Performance Guide: The Only
Reference You Need to Build a Powerful Sales Force*

A Team of Eagles

How to Manage Your Boss

The Small Business Troubleshooter

Wars of Succession

Fast Track: How To Gain and Keep Momentum

One Step Ahead: The Unused Keys to Success

Bounce Back and Win: What It Takes and How To Do It

Magnet People: Their Secrets and How To Learn From Them

*Little Things—Big Results:
How Small Events Determine Our Fate*

How to Make Your Boss Your Ally and Advocate

Building Your Legacy: One Decision At a Time

ON CD-ROM

The Personal Business Coach

Beyond Commitment: The Skills All Leaders Need

100 Ways to
Bring Out Your Best

This book was written as a
challenge ... to see if I could
honestly qualify to have this
as my epitaph:

"He gave the best that he had
for as long as he could."

100 Ways to Bring Out Your Best

Roger Fritz

Inside Advantage Publications
Naperville, Illinois

Published by:
Inside Advantage Publications
1240 Iroquois Drive, Suite 406
Naperville, IL 60563
Phone: 630-420-7673
Fax: 630-420-7835
rfritz3800@aol.com
http://www.rogerfritz.com

Unless specifically noted by naming others, all quotations are attributable to the author, Roger Fritz.

Cover and Book Design by Charles King
This book was typeset with Adobe® In Design®, using headings in Myriad®, text in Minion®.

http://www.rogerfritz.com

Inside Advantage Publications
Naperville, Illinois

Dedication

To Kate

for whom I have
always wanted
to do my best.

Acknowledgments

The work of these people was especially helpful:

— Don Young's realistic approach in researching topical coverage.

— Irene O'Neill's thorough attention to all the organizational details.

— Charles King's creative designs for cover and content.

100 Ways to Bring Out Your Best

Preface

As I consider my surroundings after over seven decades of life, three observations seem clear: 1) normal humans have a wide range of talents and abilities, 2) those who consistently fall below expectation usually have themselves to blame, 3) those who progress continuously have learned how to benefit from their strengths. Having become aware of what they do best, they are determined to keep improving.

With that conviction, I set out to identify the components of what it takes to *bring out your best*. This book is the result. My hope is that it will provide a reasonable and realistic way for readers to reexamine their own situation and assess their most appropriate options for change and progress.

The challenge is to bring future potential accomplishments into the present from day-to-day.

**We are more likely to improve
when we expect to.**

Introduction

You've heard it said: "He's his own worst enemy."

Were they talking about you?

Sometimes, it seems, we unwittingly do things that tend to work against us. Naïve? Perhaps. Dumb? Sometimes. And sometimes it's just an indication of a well-intended act that has somehow gone bad.

In my 30 years as a management consultant, I have seen thousands of such situations. Sometimes, they were minor . . . and simply overlooked. In some cases, however, the result was virtually career-ending for the individual involved.

Because the stakes can be so high it makes good sense to reexamine our behavior, to see whether and how we may be blocking our own pathway to success.

It's easy for people to say things like . . .

"He got what he deserved."
"She never had a chance."
"He handicapped himself from the beginning."
"What can you expect from someone like her?"
"The deck was stacked against him."

Unfortunately, most of the education and training designed to stimulate us to improve is based on the assumption: that we will *always* try to be at our best. The truth is: we *rarely* are at our best. We seem to live day after day in a survival mode. Why? Why do we settle for so much less than our capability? Why is our potential not reached? Why do we consistently fall short of what we might have achieved?

The best answer, it seems to me, is that we are not aware of the core issues involved. Even worse, we have not learned to use the available tools at our disposal – tools that can continuously elevate our accomplishments.

That is the purpose of this book. Its successes will depend on whether it opens up some very specific ways to help you move forward. None are absolute. None are guaranteed. None are automatic. And certainly none will come without concentrated thought and effort.

There is no doubt in my mind that those who apply themselves to understanding them and applying them conscientiously will benefit far beyond their original hope.

—Roger Fritz

1

Think Ahead

**An obstacle in your mind is worse
than an obstacle on your path.
If you think you can't, you can't.**

---

1. Create Your Future

Planning is the process by which we continuously create our own future. It is not a mental exercise, a method of forecasting, or even a systematic recording of past data from which you can attempt to predict future events. It is the approach used to turn expectations into realities.

Few things receive as much lip service – and as little action – as planning. We put it off because it requires digging for information, or because associates can't agree. Often, the thought of formulating a new plan causes panic among those who "don't want to rock the boat." But most of all we hesitate because trying to anticipate the future requires us to THINK! The benefits of planning far outweigh any inconveniences or frustrations that may be involved. A well-developed plan should:

- Relate individual objectives to overall goals of the organization or group.
- Offer a means of measuring costs, time involvement, people requirements, and other essential information.
- Identify problems and obstacles as well as benefits and opportunities.
- Suggest the most effective schedule to obtain results in the shortest period of time.

A good plan works backwards from the ultimate objective to the specific current action needed. Unless that happens you never really focus on the jobs that are most important.

2. Begin at the Beginning

**The right answers require
the right questions.**

The first and most important step in planning is to carefully analyze your present position by asking, "*Where are we now?*" This will help you to determine:

- Problems that must be resolved before any other action can be taken.
- Opportunities that haven't been noticed (or present) in the past.
- Competitive factors that could prevent you from reaching your objectives.
- New prospects that can contribute to growth.
- Previous mistakes or oversights that have proved costly.

Avoid guesswork. The plan you develop can be no better than the sources you have used, and resources available. Factor in your personal contacts, requests from customers and prospects, product or service applications, complaints, changes that have had to be made, demographic studies, and computer-stored data.

Once the information has been gathered, it must be organized to be useful. Check it for accuracy. Be sure it's complete. Arrange the information in its order of importance. Compare it with information previously available. Then outline actions to be taken.

See both immediate and long-term goals. Be sure they are realistic ... specific ... and achievable. Will they bring about the desired changes? Can they be realized within a reasonable period of time and with a reasonable cost of time, money and people? Do they specify *who* is responsible for *what* and by *when*? Are your new objectives sufficiently challenging, helping the company to overcome any foreseeable problems and seize any available opportunities? Can they contribute significantly to growth, revenues, profits, market share, and return on investment?

Your plan should establish checkpoints to insure staying on schedule, and identify alternate courses of action, should the need arise. When properly prepared, your action plan should:

- generate agreement on the part of those who will be involved
- ensure fewer false starts
- improve teamwork
- allow fewer and less-severe errors to occur
- eliminate the misassignment of responsibilities

The steps should be logical. The proper people should be involved. The deadlines should be reasonable.

3. Stay on Target

The best plans are flexible and evaluated continuously. They must be modified to meet changing conditions.

These questions will help to guide you in testing your ideas or plans:

- If fully implemented, what are the ultimate benefits of this idea?
- Does it conflict with any other objectives?
- What are the barriers? Can I eliminate them myself or do I need help?
- Who else needs to be involved?
- Do I have the resources needed to do the job? If not, where will I get them?

To ensure realistic workloads for those involved in your plan, prepare a schedule. Reasonably anticipate the amount of time needed. Then:

- Be sure your objectives are being met on schedule.
- Identify, evaluate and remedy problems that cause delays.
- Make future deadlines realistic.
- Keep everyone informed of progress.

4. Develop Reliable Sources of Information

Let your hook be always cast; in the pool where you least expect it, there may be a fish.
—Ovid, 43 BC – 17 AD

There are a number of ways in which you can obtain the valuable information you need to keep your business on course. For example, you can:

- **Conduct surveys,** either in person or by mail, primarily among your most important customer groups. From them, you can learn new or better ways to get business.

- **Attend workshops,** generally on very specific topics where you have a need for special expertise or experience.
- **Go to conventions and trade shows,** where you can see the newest equipment, visit with your peers, listen to experts talking about special subject areas, or make contact with potential suppliers.

5. Analyze Objectively

Leaders in whom we have the most confidence are objective (vs. subjective). They aren't afraid of facts and don't try to hide them. Leaders typically have four characteristics in common.

1. They spend time with people who don't focus on the past. They discipline themselves to look forward, not back. They gather facts about "what is" vs. "what was."
2. They look for trends. They differentiate between fads which are fleeting and developments that are likely to last. They listen to opinions but are much more interested in facts.
3. They are ready, willing and able to reexamine their biases. They associate with people who challenge them. They explore new alternatives. They seek new information and share it.
4. They are super-sensitive to "spin." They recognize the ways politicians and others avoid issues where they are vulnerable and reverse answers to make them look good. They realize that those who use personal attacks usually have a weak case on the issues.

6. Choose Advisors Carefully

The challenge is to find ways to obtain reliable information before a decision must be made. The objective is not so much finding people who will tell you what you must do as it is to find people who can intelligently help evaluate options. Above all, avoid "Get Rich Quick Schemes." Here's a good example:

Joe Gibbs reached the pinnacle of success as a coach when his Washington Redskins won the 1983 Super Bowl. But his elation was short lived. Not long after, he made a series of bad investments resulting in huge debts he could not repay. Finally, with help from friends and encouragement from his wife and sons, debts were paid. The family now operates a very successful and profitable car racing business.

Lesson: Why sacrifice good things for high-risk ventures? Lasting financial success comes from persistence and doing what you do best.

7. Tap Into Experience

The most successful people get the help they need *before* they need it. They find knowledgeable people, and tap their experience and insight. It's important though, to avoid getting too many people involved.

"Groupthink" has some potential hazards. Beware of these:

- Occasionally, everyone will get along so well there will be no disagreement. No one will speak the truth for fear of disrupting the harmony within the group or offending another person.
- A group may choose to rationalize reasons to delay, rather than recognize the need to take corrective action.
- Instead of seeking innovative ideas they may take the easy way and fall back on "safe" alternatives.
- Polarization may occur between those for and those against the group's decisions. This is very difficult to deal with because you run the risk of being seen as "playing favorites" no matter which side you take.

The best route is to base your decisions on facts. Avoid making assumptions. Above all, select people whose talents, experience and interests supplement your own.

8. Become Your Own Critic

Not *all* advice is *good* advice. Not *all* criticism is *good* criticism. But it is also true that buried *somewhere* in the criticism and advice you seek there is a hint . . . a trace . . . a suggestion . . . that there is something you might be able to do better than you are doing it now. The key is to become your own critic. Here's how.

The next time you face a problem you want to blame on someone else, ask a close friend about it. Tell them first you do not want them to endorse your conclusions but to give you the truth as they see it. Then brace yourself and prepare for the discomfort which may follow. Or better still, become your own critic. Ask yourself: Am I being honest about this? What have I overlooked? Why am I so angry? What are the consequences if I stay on this track?

The more you can depend on yourself to be objective the better your decisions will be.

A good example is the Sheraton Hotel chain. They have been a mainstay of the hotel business for years. Recently, though, they developed a reputation for poor customer service and facilities. So what did they do to correct it? They offered financial reimbursement to dissatisfied customers. What's the message? "We know we're bad, but we want your business anyway, so we'll pay you for your inconvenience." Marketing expert Celia Rock says, "But most Sheratons are clean, conveniently located and a good value. These are things they can build on, things that are far more worthy of highlighting than their weaknesses."

Being your own critic means being aware of both your strengths and weaknesses. But it doesn't necessarily mean pointing out your weaknesses to everyone. It does mean building on your strengths, continuing to improve and emphasizing them.

9. Anticipate Changes Needed

The best leaders have 2 qualities in common: 1) they recognize the need for change before it's too late and 2) they are willing to make tough decisions that may not be popular, but are needed to move forward.

The opposite is also true. Those who procrastinate or avoid decisions find that competitors have taken over,

technology has passed them by, or key people have re-
signed and moved on.

The skills required to anticipate the need for change are
not complex. The process is quite simple. We take an idea,
add to it, take something away, or change assumptions.

Here is a trustworthy sequence of steps that has worked
for me.

1. **Name the objective.** What's the problem? What kind
   of ideas do you need? Use quantitative terms, such as
   time, dollars or units. State your primary and secondary
   objectives.

2. **Get the facts.** Gather all the information you can
   about the problem, including unsuccessful attempts
   to solve it. Often, an idea that has failed in one set of
   circumstances can be highly successful in another.

3. **Brainstorm.** Line up your alternatives. Make no attempt to evaluate or prioritize them; simply try to list
   as many as you can.

4. **Try the obvious solutions first.** Often, a simple solution
   may result simply by following steps 1 and 2. Consider
   the short-term and long-term consequences of each
   action. Be specific and, again, try to use quantitative
   terms. Are the necessary resources available?

5. **Try the wild ideas.** Look, in particular, for the appar-
   ently trivial, irrelevant aspects of the problem.

6. **Think intensely about the problem.** Actually, this is
   not a separate step, but a part of all the previous steps.
   Make yourself think about the problem until you either
   reach a solution or reach a state of frustration.

7. **Walk away from the problem.** Put the problem out
   of your mind for a while. Sometimes, distancing

yourself from the problem allows your subconscious to take over.

8. **Seize the final flash of insight.** Generally, at some indefinite time after you have walked away from the problem, you will find an answer beginning to take form in your mind. Grab it and write it down.

9. **Do something about the idea.** Don't get discouraged. Above all, don't give up. Persistence and determination can eventually direct you to some amazing results.

10. **Sell Your Decisions.**

Your best decisions enable you to look forward to getting up each morning.

Having selected the best course of action to be taken, test your decision. Discuss it with key associates and those who will be most directly affected by it. Try to draw out any obstacles or objections and have a backup plan ready. But remember, when you announce your decision, you *must* be prepared to sell it by 1) presenting the facts as you see them, 2) pointing out the weaknesses you found in other plans, 3) responding to all known objections and explaining how they will be met, 4) detailing the benefits, and 5) finding new believers and advocates. By word and action, let it be known that you are committed to your decision, and to making it work.

If it is possible to test your ideas before you go full-scale, do it. Be prepared to make some unexpected modifications or corrections.

Some problems may seem to defy solution, no matter how hard you try. Beware of these hazards:

- Some people may be hesitant to criticize you and are telling you what they think you want to hear rather than revealing their true feelings.
- Urgency often stimulates unreliable judgment.
- Persistent conflicts may be working against a constructive and cooperative solution.
- Those who feel responsible for creating or contributing to a problem are protecting themselves.
- People are looking at the situation only from their own viewpoints.
- Resistance to change is creating tension, fear and uncertainty.

You can overcome these tendencies if you are able to bring out your best.

2

Believe *You Can*

**Self-confidence is built
only by breaking away from routine.**

The first question to ask when facing a new challenge is "Do I believe I can?" . . . If the answer is yes, the second question is "Why do I think so?" And then, "What steps must I take?" This requires a candid self-appraisal that is as honest and objective as it can be. The process starts with you. No one else can change your behavior – especially if it has become habitual.

11. Examine Yourself

If you can't appraise yourself objectively, the chance of accurately appraising others is very low. Consider it to be your responsibility to make your performance appraisal as useful and beneficial as possible. Try these steps to get the most out of the experience.

- A week before your review, take the time to perform a thorough appraisal on yourself. List what you have done well, but also note mistakes and where you might have done better. Think about specific things you will need to do to improve.
- Practice talking aloud about your strengths, as well as the areas you would like to change and why.
- During the actual review, get all of the information you can about the good and the bad. If you're unsure ask, "Could you be more specific?"
- Keep a level head. Use criticism as an indication of an area in which you might need to improve.
- Follow up. Measure your own achievements and ask about progress, especially in the areas associated with previous criticism.

12. Recognize the Causes of "Flame-Out"

We limit our ability to bring out our best when we are discouraged. The first place to look when enthusiasm and ambition lag is inside yourself. Ask why do I feel this way? What has changed? Consider these possibilities:

- Your personal goals and the goals of your organization are too far apart.

- You are mired down in repetitive, unchallenging, boring work.
- You need new forms of expertise and influence.
- Your personal objectives have changed.
- Your skills have diminished, perhaps through lack of use.
- You receive inadequate recognition for your contributions – a common complaint among high achievers.

The only way to restore your energy and full capability is to evaluate each of these possibilities honestly and thoroughly. For instance, if you believe your skills are outdated ask which ones. How? Why? What new skills must I have? How will I get them? Where? When?

13. Don't Play the Blame Game

**The plea of the non-performer is,
"It wasn't my fault" — beware all who use it.**

If you find yourself being blamed for many things by many people one of the best responses I have found is to say simply, "OK – Blame me."

Blame Me

—If you think I'm pushing you to bring out
   your best – Blame Me!
—If you are resisting the changes you know
   you must make – Blame Me!
—If you don't want to meet some of the
   deadlines you are facing – Blame Me!
—If you are afraid to take a risk because it
   might not work – Blame Me!
—If you find yourself avoiding
   accountability – Blame Me!
—If you are usually late and miss needed
   information – Blame Me!
—If you take the easy way and lose – Blame Me!
—If you are not prepared for an
   advancement and don't get it – Blame Me!
—If you consistently devote most of your
   time to low priorities – Blame Me!
—If you are too tired to meet your daily
   responsibilities – Blame Me!

Then, when all of the blame is transferred
to me, you can ask yourself, "Why isn't Roger
making things better for me? Isn't he strong
enough, smart enough, or influential enough?
If not – why not?"

Blame me if you want to. But please, when
your life improves long-term, take the credit
yourself because only you could make it happen. As for me – my reward will come from
helping you.

14. Reduce Job Stress

Job stress can erode efficiency, productivity, and even mental and physical health. It is one of the principle factors leading to burn-out. Try this quiz to see how much job-related stress you have now.

If the statement *never* applies to you, give yourself a score of 1. If it *seldom* applies to you, take a 2. If it *sometimes* applies to you, it's a 3; *often* applies to you, a 4; and *always* applies to you, a 5.

1. I'm not sure what's expected of me. _____
2. Others' demands for my time are in conflict. _____
3. Commuting to and from work is a constant headache. _____
4. Management regularly expects me to interrupt my work for new priorities. _____
5. I have a poor relationship with my boss. _____
6. I only receive feedback when my performance is unsatisfactory. _____
7. There is little chance for promotion in my organization. _____
8. Decisions and changes that affect me are made without my knowledge. _____
9. I have to work under crowded or noisy conditions. _____
10. I have too much to do and too little time to do it. _____
11. I feel uncomfortable with the political climate of the organization. _____
12. I do not have enough work to do. _____

13. The fear of failure is constantly on my mind.   _____
14. I'm not sure I am qualified for my job.   _____
15. I'm afraid someone else is getting ready to
    take over my job.   _____
16. I feel pressures from home about my work
    hours.   _____
17. I spend my time fighting fires, rather than
    working on priorities.   _____
18. The organization is continually threatened
    by layoffs.   _____
19. I don't have the opportunity to use my
    knowledge and skills on the job.   _____
20. It seems I move from one deadline to another.   _____

TOTAL SCORE   _____

If your total score is under 50, you can relax and enjoy your work. The pressures are exceptionally few. If your score is 50-60, you're experiencing normal on-the-job stress and there's little to worry about. A score between 60 and 70 indicates a moderate amount of stress and indicates that some changes ought to be considered as soon as practical to reduce the pressure. When the score ranges between 70 and 80, you are undergoing an abnormal amount of stress and should make some changes immediately. Between 80 and 90, stress has reached the danger point; and over 90, you had better make some major changes *at once*.

15. Manage Your Own Career

Too often, people allow their careers to manage themselves. They go to work each day, try hard and trust their employer will act appropriately on their behalf.

If you don't learn to manage your own career, you place your future in someone else's hands. You are then saying in effect, *I trust you more than myself.* Here are some practical suggestions that will serve you well.

- Get a clear fix on your own capabilities and interests. Work isn't work when you are doing something you enjoy.
- Make a list of your available options. Don't fasten too firmly onto a single career objective too early in the game.
- Filter your options to set priorities. Prepare a list of alternatives and start focusing on the best.
- Decide on a lifestyle you would like to have. Some people want power ... or money ... and will pay any price to get them. Others want to be comfortable and think of a job as nothing more than a means of supporting that goal.
- Prepare a written plan to cover the next five years. What's included? Where are you now? How did you get there? If you didn't do anything different, where would you expect to be in one year? – two years? – five years?
- List the constraints and limitations.
- Devise a realistic financial plan. Start building your cash reserves, emergency funds, for retirement needs.

- Start a wellness program for physical fitness. Getting a fitness assessment at a reputable health club by professional exercise specialists is a good place to start.
- Take regular vacations to relax. Workaholics burn out quickly.
- Involve your family in your personal career plans. People who totally separate their work decisions from their personal lives usually find more stress.
- Use your weekends for a change of pace. Develop some type of hobby. It will do wonders to revitalize your outlook.
- Clarify your job objectives. Make an appointment with your boss to discuss the specific results you expect to produce and how you will measure them.
- Set aside a certain part of your day/week/month to work on improving your knowledge and your skills.

16. Appraise Applause

Those who concentrate on praise take their eyes off of what is required to win. Alvin York is a name now unfamiliar to most. Yet, he is one of our country's best examples of a person who had to adapt *totally* to a new situation and then excelled. He grew up dirt poor in the mountains of Tennessee. Born in a tiny cabin, third child of eleven, his mother did laundry for neighbors, while his father struggled to get crops from a small, hilly, rocky farm. Because he was needed to work, Alvin only made it through third grade.

York had strong religious objections to killing. Acting on them, he applied for Conscientious Objector status early in World War I. When denied, he tried four more times, but was inducted into the army in November 1917.

A sure-shot, achieved through practice hunting rabbits and wild turkeys, he could not escape killing in the army. When he committed to something, he honored it. In a crucial battle in France, York killed 25 Germans, and practically single-handedly, captured 132 more. But he was not keeping score. He was simply trying to do everything he could to shorten the war so he could go home.

When that time came he was a hero, welcomed by parades, and awarded the Distinguished Service Cross and the Congressional Medal of Honor. Sgt. York declined many lucrative offers for movie rights and product endorsements. Instead, he devoted himself to helping other poor mountain families in the Appalachians by establishing a school in his home county of Fentess, later renamed the York Agricultural Institute in his honor.

17. Change Before You Must

Change doesn't come easily . . . but it can be less troublesome if you devise ways to keep on track. Try these:

1. Think objectively. Where are you now? How did you get there? Where will you be in the future if you don't do anything differently?
2. Scan wider horizons. What changes would eliminate the threats or dangers you face?

3. Increase your visibility. To stand out from others, your goals must be higher than theirs.

4. Keep your options open. Use your best talents to create more options.

5. People who plan and prepare out-perform those who don't. To avoid unwanted surprises:
   - Become an expert at what you do.
   - Know what resources you need, as well as where and how to get them.
   - Shift those resources to get the highest yield.
   - Set up an *objective* system to measure progress.
   - Take a realistic view of the future–don't trust opinions.
   - Budget time carefully.
   - Become the best example of self-discipline.
   - Stay away from negative people.

Example: The family which owns Omaha Steaks came to realize that their high quality meat could be sold profitably in many ways. First, in stores, hotels and restaurants, then in 1963 via catalogs. Since 1990, they sell on-line and the company now ships its products to 1.5 million customers.

18. Leverage Your Abilities

**More failure results from
indecision than wrong choices.**

Almost everyone has felt a need to change directions. Maybe they believe they have reached their limit where they are. Maybe a new opportunity has opened up. Maybe they are tired of doing the same thing day after day. Whatever the motivation, when that happens, consider these three keys to focus on your strengths:

- **Expect obstacles.** Ask for criticism and feedback. If your convictions are strong enough, you will find ways to overcome any obstacles that may stand in your way. Mark Gearan, an educator, chose to become the director of the Peace Corps at a time when government service wasn't particularly popular. The job appealed to him, however, because he genuinely believed in the ability of government to help some people who are in need.
- **Don't expect miracles.** When you start from a fresh new beginning, realize that progress will take time. Stay focused on your eventual goal.
- **Refuse to settle for less than your best.** Seek responsibility. Success will come when you find a role that allows you to creatively utilize a combination of your abilities. Don't avoid what you do best. Find a balance between your talents and your interests.

Charles Kettering, founder of Delco and former Vice President of General Motors was a self-made inventor-mogul, topped only by Thomas Edison. Kettering, who held over 200 patents, was known for the electronic self-starter found in most car engines today. He was also a pioneer in the development of diesel engines, anti-knock gas, home air conditioning units, and quick-drying paint for cars.

He had little time for traditional schooling and contended that, "Overly educated people were the ones least likely to make new discoveries because they were too intent on doing things the way they had been taught."

Eyestrain was a problem for Kettering, so classmates read aloud to him, teaching him to rely on his own inner vision, giving him a better mental picture to draw from.

19. Avoid Doubters

Optimists see possibilities.
Pessimists refuse to look.

If the people who influence you most are always concerned about what can't be done, you are liable to join them. Doubters and pessimists stay the same or get worse. Avoid these "mildewed" people (afflicted by a fungus from being in the dark too long), if you believe things can be better.

In 1920, Robert Goddard, a physics professor at Clark University in Worcester, Massachusetts, wrote a paper expressing the belief that man could build a rocket capable of reaching the moon. The story appeared in newspapers throughout the world. Some of them weren't very kind. *The New York Times* and the *London Graphic*, for example, said that it was impossible for a rocket to perform in space because it would not have gravity to push against. Another paper rudely stated that Goddard lacked "the knowledge ladled out daily in high schools." He was not discouraged.

"Every vision is a joke," he announced, "until the first man accomplishes it."

To be successful in space, he knew a rocket would require a new fuel to propel it. He began to work on mixtures of liquid hydrogen and liquid oxygen. The hydrogen would propel the rocket; the oxygen would replace the air needed to keep the fuel burning.

In 1926, Goddard built and launched a 10-foot rocket that reached a speed of 60 mph, stayed in the air 2.5 seconds, and climbed to an altitude of 41 feet. Goddard was encouraged, but knew that a rocket would have to go at least 25,000 mph in order to escape Earth's gravity. He built a rocket near Roswell, New Mexico, where he sent 14-, 16-, and 18-foot rockets to altitudes of 2,000, 7,500 and 9,000 feet. One exceeded the speed of sound. Another featured some revolutionary fin-stabilized steering.

When World War II came along, Goddard's technology produced rockets for use by airplanes. Before his death in 1945, he had patented 214 items associated with rocketry. Not only was he acknowledged as a pioneer in modern rocketry, he also was – and continues to be – recognized as the father of space flight. He overcame all doubters.

20. Lean Forward and Don't Look Back

War provides few opportunities for error. Military commanders who second-guess themselves usually lose. Decisions must be made instantaneously and the stakes are very, very high. Examples set by some of history's greatest military leaders carry valuable lessons for everyone who wants to improve.

Ulysses S. Grant. Of him, President Abraham Lincoln once said: "I cannot spare this man. He fights." Told that Grant also liked to drink, Lincoln replied: "Tell me his brand so that I may send the same to all my generals." Gen. William T. Sherman added: "I know more about strategy, logistics, and every aspect of military employment than he (Grant). However, there is one aspect in which Grant beats me and everyone else. He runs into problems and they don't bother him. He keeps pressing on."

Hannibal. The Romans knew about Hannibal's plan to lead a herd of elephants through the Alps and into Rome, but they said it couldn't be done. Hannibal responded: "We will find a way or make one."

Adm. David Farragut. At the battle of Mobile Bay in August 1864, Farragut commanded a fleet of four iron-clad monitors and 14 wooden ships. As he sailed into the Confederate gunfire, a mine destroyed his leading monitor. The fleet stopped cold. Some of Farragut's officers urged him to retreat; instead, he had himself strapped to the rigging of his flagship, the *USS Hartford*, ordered his ship into the minefield, and issued the famous command: "Damn the torpedoes! Full speed ahead!"

Napoleon Bonaparte. Asked about his talent for planning and thinking ahead, Napoleon replied: "If I always appear prepared, it is because, before entering an undertaking, I have thought a long time and tried to foresee what may occur. It is not genius which reveals to me suddenly and secretly what I should do in circumstances unexpected by others. It is meditation and preparation."

**Courageous people look fear
in the face and say, "bring it on."**

There's a better way to do it. Find it!

—Thomas Edison

3

First Things First

21. Know Your Strengths

Winners discover a way to stand out among the competition. The easiest way to do that is to play to your strengths.

Singer Neil Diamond takes his songs personally. If they don't mirror his feelings and emotions, he says, they won't be any good.

"The main objective in any song I write," says Diamond, "has always been that it reflects the way I feel. That it touches me when I'm finished with it and involves me in what it's saying. And that's really the only rule I use when writing."

In all, Diamond has 31 gold albums, making him second only to Elvis Presley among male solo artists in that category.

When fans flock to Diamond's concerts, they feel he's one of them, giving voice to the things they feel themselves.

It is surprising, then, to learn that Diamond nearly didn't make it in the music business.

After writing songs through high school and college, he achieved his first copyright in 1960 for a song called *What Will I Do?* His next few years were like a roller coaster. He associated with several publishers, including Columbia Records, but he couldn't sustain a long-term relationship. He became frustrated, but he didn't give up.

Diamond eventually decided that he had been trying too hard to write songs for other people's tastes. He began to compose and sing songs that satisfied his own feelings and desires.

"I began, for the first time, to write songs that I wanted to write, that I felt, that moved me, that I cared about," says Diamond. "And it became exciting to me again. I felt that there was no more necessity for me to fail, that I could do what I wanted."

And so he did.

22. Don't Look for Security

**To expect security
is to take a holiday from history.**

When people place security as their highest priority, the results are scary. For example, almost nobody gets fired from a federal government civil service job. Regulations shield incompetent and negligent employees so that only 5 State Department employees out of 28,000 were fired in

16 years (1984 – 2000). The process can take 18 months or longer. Meanwhile they continue to be paid and are obviously resented by those whose workload increases.

Those who bring out their best put themselves in competitive situations and do not depend upon artificial regulations, quotas or tenure. The only security is what you create for yourself.

The perfect bureaucrat is the man who manages to make no decisions and escapes all responsibility.

—Brooks Atkinson, drama critic, essayist

Too many people count on somebody else to tell them how they are doing and what they should do to improve. You will get a jump on your competition if 1) you are honest with yourself about your own basic behavior and 2) you learn to initiate action for change on your own, without depending on others to do it for you.

The first step in this process is to evaluate your self-confidence level. Ask yourself these questions:

- Am I goal oriented? Am I dedicated to reaching the goals that I have established?
- Do I demonstrate self-reliance or, in times of stress or crisis, do I back away?
- Do I use a creative approach to reach decisions or solutions to problems, or do I rely on old ways with which I feel comfortable?

- Do people usually trust my decisions?
- Do people tend to assist me willingly?
- Do people usually react positively to my suggestions?
- Do I make an honest effort to encourage feedback from others?
- Do I continue doing a good job even when there is no *immediate* reward?
- Do I support those who must help carry out decisions I made?
- Am I optimistic? Do I bounce back quickly?
- Do I feel like I am in good health?

If most of your answers are "yes," you tend to see yourself in a positive light and are in a good position to begin the deliberate process of building a personal progress plan for yourself.

23. Pace Your Race

The Ohio River flows at a speed of eight miles per hour. If you are standing beside the river and decide to jump in, you know you'll be moving at that speed.

The lesson: If you don't want to travel at that pace, find a slower river. Or better still, a lake.

When you go too fast you may burn out quickly. When you go too slow you may never be a contender. Two basic principles are involved in pacing your race:

1. Failure is determined by what you allow to happen; success by what you make happen. Keep your cool. Control your emotions in reaching tough decisions. Before you blow your top in public, talk it out with yourself. Reduce anxieties by acting out the situation alone. Ask yourself: What's the worst that can happen? Then let your answer guide your actions.

Another benefit: You avoid the tendency to run others down or place blame irresponsibly. None of this happens by chance. A negative approach puts the brakes on progress.

2. Success and failure have the same root: the desire to achieve. But avoiding failure is not the same as success.

Knowing how far you've traveled on the road to success is the first major step. An effective way to pinpoint your current position is to answer these questions:

- What are my major strengths?
- What weaknesses have I identified that may inhibit my progress?
- What have been my major achievements in the past 30 days? The last quarter? The last six months? The last year?
- What did I learn in the past year that will help me most in the future?
- Who, other than myself, contributed significantly to the accomplishment of my objectives? Have I thanked them?
- What outside factors influenced my success or failure?

Once you understand where you are, it is possible to establish more realistic, specific objectives based upon what you have learned about yourself and the work you must do.

To move in the right direction, your objectives must meet these tests:

- *They must be realistic.* Can they be achieved within a reasonable length of time? What costs are involved?
- *They must be specific.* Do they specify when results can be expected? Do they state what results are being sought?
- *They must ensure improvement.* Are they a challenge? Will they overcome problems and capitalize on opportunities?

When you have selected a destination, the next step is to select a route to get you there. Being prepared is more important than speed. Write down the objectives you have established. Prepare a written, step-by-step outline of actions you plan to take. Give yourself a time limit. Estimate the costs. Determine the type and amount of support required.

The vital phase of a plan for success is the action phase. Not only does it provide a clear-cut route to your objectives, it helps to minimize the chances for error.

To keep your plan on course, it is important to check for changes needed, or new opportunities requiring immediate attention. Then you must act!

24. Protect Your Health

**Take time to be fit or make time
to be sick ... your choice.**

All of the success in the world means nothing unless you have the good health to enjoy it. We are endangering ourselves at an alarming rate. Consider these startling facts: About 15.9 million people, or 7% of the population used illegal drugs in '01, says a government survey. That's an 18% jump. Marijuana, cocaine and pain relievers are on the rise. Teen use rose to 10.8% from 9.7%.

I was shocked recently in a conversation with my pharmacist who said I would be surprised by how many of his adult customers were on Prozac and kids were on Ritalin.

Why can't we cope without using drugs to help us face everyday problems? The first step is control what we can control.

Here's a quick way to check danger signals:

- Do you smoke?
- Is your blood pressure 160/90 or above?
- Is your total blood cholesterol level above 200 mg/dl?
- Is your HDL cholesterol level below 35 mg/dl?
- Are you physically inactive or overweight?
- Is your diet high in cholesterol and saturated fat?

- Is your diet lacking in whole grains, fruit and vegetables?
- Do you have a family history of heart disease?
- Are you impatient and hostile in everyday situations?

The more "yes" answers you have, the greater your risk of heart disease and the greater your need to start a program to reduce that risk now.

25. Beat the Odds

Never take advantage of people.

—J.C. Penney

Many people go through life defensively. They are trying not to get hurt. Unfortunately, life is *hard*. Attempting to achieve something, to get ahead, to make something of yourself makes it even harder ... but the results are usually worth it.

What kind of person must you be in order to beat the odds? These clues, I believe, have the greatest promise:

- Select your friends carefully – choose those who are assets, not liabilities.
- Be careful whom you learn from – bad company attracts bad company.
- Listen to those who love you – they have the greatest stake in your success.

- Know before you talk – words before thought can be dangerous.
- Don't experiment with values – values are constant not relative.
- Don't curse adversity – there is great benefit in working your way out of tough times.
- Never substitute excuses for hard work – excuse makers are not trusted.
- Learn where to find out the things you don't know – memory alone is not trustworthy.
- Never compromise morals – it's the surest way to lower yourself.
- Respect only those who earn it – the world is full of good actors and actresses.
- Make persistence your legacy – most regrets are due to giving up too soon.
- Don't delay – perform – procrastinators never know their potential.

26. Focus on Priorities

Above all, successful people T H I N K. They don't "assume," "hope" or "expect" without serious analysis. Here's a good illustration. A teacher pulled out a one-gallon jar and set it on the desk in front of him. When the jar was filled to the top with rocks, he asked, "Is the jar full?" Everyone said "Yes."

He then dumped some gravel in and shook the jar. The gravel filled the spaces between the rocks. Then he asked, "Is the jar full? By this time the class was onto him. "Probably not," they answered. He then started dumping in sand, and it went into all the spaces between the rocks and the gravel. Once more he asked, "Is this jar full?" "No!" the class shouted. He next poured water in until the jar was filled to the brim. Then he asked, "What is the point of this?"

Lesson: Ask yourself what are the "big rocks" (priorities) in my personal life and career? Am I putting them in the jar first?

What kind of people are most likely to seize an opportunity once it opens up? Typically it is those who are:

- Dissatisfied – they are always looking for improvement.
- Creative – they believe there are better ways.
- Aggressive – they don't stay on the sidelines.
- Insightful – they look beyond the obvious.
- Risk-takers – they don't expect gain without pain.
- Communicators – they make sure they are understood.
- Diligent – their brain rests only when they sleep.
- Persistent – they sometimes fall back but rarely give up.
- Resilient – they bounce back quickly.
- Self-confident – they are prepared.
- Unselfish – they share credit where it is due.

27. Don't Punish Yourself

Too many people handicap themselves. When that is allowed to happen they diminish their potential and are never competitive. The key is to acknowledge mistakes and move forward.

We punish ourselves and become our own worst enemy when:

- We tolerate below-par results for too long.
- We fail to define what performance means.
- We tend to over-manage talented, competent people.
- We don't know our own strengths and how to capitalize on them at work.
- We are blinded by the weaknesses of others and don't know what their strengths might be.
- We reward busyness, seniority, credentials, political behavior, and clones.
- We don't build on accountable people.
- We allow status abusers to continue.
- We punish initiative and risk-takers.
- We resist empowering others.
- We don't rejoice in the success of others.
- We seek to complicate, not simplify.

Fortunately, these need not be permanent or fatal. Here are the time-tested remedies:

- Solicit participation in planning.
- Rely on facts and objective evidence of progress, not opinions.
- Commit goals in writing.
- Always determine *who* will do *what* by *when.*
- Select those who show persistence.
- Negotiate clear, objective performance contracts.
- Avoid email or memo wars. Talk frequently.
- Encourage dissent and constructive criticism.
- Avoid shooting the bearers of bad news.

- Criticize privately, but praise publicly.
- Don't reward those who resist change.
- Reward results as opposed to activities, and effectiveness as opposed to efficiency.

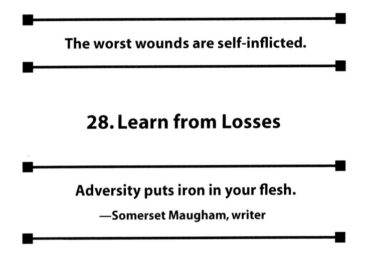

The worst wounds are self-inflicted.

28. Learn from Losses

Adversity puts iron in your flesh.

—Somerset Maugham, writer

Longtime victory only comes to those who learn the most from losses. Nowhere is that more apparent than in professional sports, and nobody typifies that spirit more than quarterback Brett Favre and cartoonist Bill Mauldin.

In 1965, after being slammed to the ground countless times by defensive linemen, Favre became addicted to the pain-killer Vicodin. He would take 15 pills a night, and stop only two days before a game. As soon as the game was over, he would return to the pills. Vomiting and not eating became a regular part of his life. Pressured by his family and friends, he made a decision. He entered a rehabilitation program, where he stayed for six weeks, and gave up alcohol as well as Vicodin.

Favre was named the NFL's Most Valuable Player a record three consecutive years, 1995, 1996 and 1997. He also played in 141 straight games – another record for NFL quarterbacks. "I may get knocked down a lot . . . but I'll always get back up again," he says.

Bill Mauldin was a smart aleck, rebellious kid who was expelled from high school for his pranks. He loved to draw, so to help his folks, at age 13, he borrowed $20 from his grandmother and took a course for cartooning. To get experience, he illustrated anything from restaurant menus to political posters and gag cartoons. While in the Army in WWII, he gave his superiors a hard time, and created the Willie and Joe cartoons. Soldiers loved its accuracy in portraying their plight. General Dwight Eisenhower overruled General George Patton who wanted Mauldin's cartoons stopped. History judged him wisely. He received two Pulitzer Prizes and was buried in Arlington National Cemetery with a 21 gun salute.

29. Test New Skills

Have you ever had an idea for a product, but shrugged it off, thinking that if there were a market for it, someone else would already have invented it? You may have given up a tremendous opportunity for success.

Two Canadian journalists, Chris Haney and Scott Abbot, seized their opportunity in the late 1970s. Because it had been 50 years since the last successful board game was introduced, most people thought they were a thing of the past.

Haney and Abbot ignored those doubts, spent five months developing a new board game, and introduced *Trivial Pursuit*.

At the Canadian Toy and Decoration Fair, only 200 of the games were sold. At the American International Toy Fair in New York City, only 144 orders were received. The box was too big. The game's design needed work. The game was too expensive.

But Haney and Abbot didn't give up. They sent the game to as many newspapers and magazines as they could afford. They also sent it to a number of celebrities, most of whom were mentioned in the questions that had been written into the game. Johnny Carson talked about the game enthusiastically on *The Tonight Show* . . . and sales began to take off.

In 1984, 20 million games were sold in the United States alone.

The gap between mediocrity and excellence is the difference measured by two things – indifference and determination.

---

30. Deserve Respect

Win my competition and I'll give you a trophy.
Win my trust and I'll give you my loyalty.

Nobody believes it's better to work for a smart person who's emotionally unstable than to work for one who's on an even keel. Studies from nearly 500 companies around the world have shown that 85 percent of what distinguishes an outstanding leader from an average one is something *other* than their technical expertise. The key factor has been identified as "emotional intelligence" or plain old compassion.

"Emotional intelligence" is composed of two parts: personal competence and social competence.

Those with personal competence are self-aware. If they are able to read their emotions, assess their strengths and limits, and act in a self-confident way, their emotional intelligence is said to be high. They are able to manage themselves well. They're in control.

Social competence suggests a person who is quite sensitive to the inner world of others. They are socially aware. They are empathic. They realize that when pride becomes arrogance, followers disappear.

Successful leaders know how to manage relationships. Are you influential, a motivator and a catalyst for change? Do you build others up, create a web of relationships, and build teams well? If so, you're demonstrating a high level of emotional intelligence and will deserve respect.

Can you keep destructive emotions in check? Are you trustworthy and flexible? Are you driven to improve performance, ready to act when needed, and optimistic in the face of difficulties? If so, you have the capability to become a successful leader.

Live in such a way that you would not be ashamed to sell your parrot to the town gossip.

—Will Rogers, actor and humorist

4

Beyond Commitment

**Mediocrity is contagious,
but so is excellence.**

—Charles Sykes

31. Earn Reliability

The mission determines the coalition.

—Donald Rumsfeld, Secretary of Defense,
regarding the US and Afghanistan

In other words, build the team most capable of accomplishing what must be done. It's much easier to explore alternatives and talk freely when you have confidence in those from whom you are seeking advice. Feelings of doubt and isolation are hard to resolve. The best cure is to get advice from people you trust. But how do you establish a trusting relationship?

A good way to start is to earn confidence by assuring your support, listening to them, helping them recognize their strengths and weaknesses and giving them constructive criticism when needed. Only then are they likely to explore new territory.

Here are key questions to help you get on the same wavelength as the people whose support you need. Do you . . .

. . . empower people to perform?

- Do they understand your intentions? If you answered *yes*, you tend to keep in close touch. Your job is easier because everyone knows what is expected.
- Do you encourage people to use plans and goals as a basis for their day-to-day work? (A *yes* indicates that you probably benefit from measurable results and quick feedback.)
- Do they get information from you soon enough to make intelligent decisions about their work? (If you answered *no*, check your personal communication network for holes. Locate the gaps and seal them.)
- Do you encourage communication and cooperation? (If the answer is *yes*, give some recent examples to prove you're right.)
- Is there evidence that you honestly encourage individual initiative? (Even if you answered *yes*, run a continuous check. So many say they encourage initiative but don't.)
- Can they ask questions without fear of a putdown? (If you answered *no*, remember that questions are

the quickest way to learn whether they understand what they need to know.)

...encourage individual results?

- Are the results you expect precisely defined? Are those results rewarded when achieved? (If you can honestly answer *yes*, chances are people are highly motivated and productive.
- Are salaries fair? Competitive? Related to performance? (A *no* means you're inviting rapid turnover.)
- Do the people who must do the work participate in setting goals? (If *yes*, it's a good bet they find their jobs satisfying and require less pushing along the way.)

...develop team support?

- Are people frank with each other? Are they afraid to tell the truth? Is information shared? (If you answered *yes*, what is your evidence? Would the people involved agree with your answer? If you answered *no*, open up!)
- When there's a problem, do you attempt to solve it on your own? (If you answered *yes*, start inviting others to share in finding a solution. The more ideas available, the quicker a sticky problem can be solved.)
- Is it difficult for you to be silent and listen to what others have to say? (A *yes* means you will have problems motivating others until they believe you really understand what they're telling you.)
- Do you urge people to express their ideas and suggestions? (If the answer is *yes*, you're in good shape – as long as they are also willing to assume responsibility for their recommendations.)

- When people make mistakes, do you usually censure them? (*Yes* means you are losing a great opportunity to use mistakes as a learning experience.

. . . make effective decisions?

- Do you think your role in the organization is clearly understood? (If you answered *no*, put your functions and responsibilities in writing. Then meet with key people to get their feedback.)
- Do you prefer to involve people in setting their goals? (If your answer is *yes*, be sure they know your priorities and expectations so they don't spend valuable time on things that don't matter to you.)
- Do you carefully consider the other person's point of view? (*Yes* means you are inviting new ideas, procedures, and techniques that otherwise would lie dormant.)
- Are you often surprised by your own decisions? (A *no* means that much of your success is likely due to careful preparation, planning and follow-through.)
- Are the objectives you establish usually realistic? Workable? Specific? (Even if you answered *yes*, make it a habit to carefully monitor your objectives to ensure that the results they promise are realized.)

Success is more satisfying when it is shared with the people who helped you achieve it.

32. Be Careful Who You Follow

Anyone who needs a ready-made model for sound moral behavior today need look no further than the virtues cited by Benjamin Franklin. Although he recognized that they are not easily attained, I believe they are as valid now as then.

Temperance — "Eat not to dullness, drink not to elevation," Franklin advised. In this age of health foods and corporate fitness programs, it is apparent that this is still very relevant today.

Silence — "When we don't listen carefully to our business associates or family members, relationships wither all around us."

Order — "Let all your things have their places; let each part of your business have its time," said Franklin, the founder of the American Philosophical Society and the University of Pennsylvania, who somehow found the time to establish a circulating library, organize the federal postal system, and build the first business franchise (a string of printing shops).

Resolution — "Resolve to perform what you ought; perform without fail what you resolve." In today's terms I call this Performance Based Management (PBM).

Frugality — "Make no unnecessary expense. Waste nothing." Excessive use of credit is a sure-fire route to disaster.

Industry — "Lose no time with unrealistic expectations." Concentrate on the highest priorities.

Sincerity — Sincerity of manner and genuine interest draws people to you. Speaking unclearly turns people off.

Justice — If you lose something, replace it. If you break something, fix it or get it fixed. Don't be careless with the property, or the rights of other people.

Moderation — You can gauge the size of a person by the size of the conflict it takes to get them angry.

Cleanliness — Appearance counts.

Tranquility — "Be not disturbed at trifles, or at accidents common or unavoidable," said Ben. Over-reacting to an event doesn't make the event go away, it merely makes the response less likely to succeed.

Humility — The world of business and politics can be a massive ego trip. The danger stems from the fact that a giant ego, incapable of listening to the truth, can cripple the organization.

You may not agree with all of Benjamin Franklin's "virtues," but you can use them as a starting point to prepare your own three-point plan for self-development.

STEP #1 – Make your own list of areas for self-development.

STEP #2 – Put your self-development targets in writing.

STEP #3 – Work on attaining your targets one at a time until you are satisfied that you have achieved your best in each area.

33. Build Your Credibility

In calm water every ship has a good captain.
—Grover Cleveland, 22nd and 24th U.S. President

Building credibility means more than simply handling major issues believably. It means doing the little things right as well. By building trust in small ways, you'll have more receptive response on the big issues.

"When I face a tough decision," says Frieda Caplan, CEO and Founder of Frieda's Finest, a California distributor of fruits and vegetables, "I ask my employees, 'What would you do if you were me?'" This approach, says Caplan, generates good ideas and introduces the employees to the complexity of making management decisions.

The objective is to gain agreement from your associates – to get them used to saying *yes*. One way to do that is to start with simple issues and relatively indisputable decisions, then gradually work your way into the more controversial matters.

As your responsibility increases ask yourself the following questions:

- How do I respond to bad news? Do I ever have a tendency to punish the messenger?
- Do I usually try to find someone to blame when things go wrong? (If so, information sources will dry up.)

- Do I differentiate between constructive suggestions and whining or undocumented complaints?
- Do most people believe I will take action when necessary and not delay?

Remember – credibility cannot be inherited or transferred. It must be earned.

34. Pull Your Way Up

Those who keep trying can renew themselves.

Expecting lasting success to come quickly is foolish. Most often, it involves starting at the bottom of the ladder and working your way up, rung by rung. The case of baseball great Eddie Matthews is a good example.

After graduating from high school in Santa Barbara, California, 17-year-old Matthews received two offers to play professional baseball. One came from the Brooklyn Dodgers and included a $60,000 signing bonus. The other came from the Boston Braves and carried a $4,000 bonus.

Matthews weighed the two options. If he went with the Dodgers, he would get more money and immediately be on the roster of a big league team. If he went with the Braves, he would get less money and would be expected to start out on one of the Braves' minor league teams.

Matthews realized that he was young and that he had a great deal to learn. He felt that starting in the minor leagues would be the best way to do that . . . and he accepted the Braves' contract. It was a wise decision.

In the minors, Matthews played with and against many former major league stars whose careers were winding down. By hanging around with them on and off the field, he learned some of the key ingredients to success: play hard, be humble, and do whatever it takes to win.

During his career, Eddie Matthews hit 512 home runs, tying Ernie Banks for 13th on the all-time career home run list. He hit 30 or more home runs in nine straight seasons – a record – and hit 40 or more home runs *four times*. He played in 10 All Star games.

In 1978, Eddie Matthews was inducted into the National Baseball Hall of Fame.

A recent study at the University of Minnesota concluded that young people who have part-time jobs in their teens have an advantage later in life. The reasons can be traced to lessons they learned involving time, budgeting, money management, interpersonal skills and handling work stress.

35. Rework Mistakes

Most experts believe that Richard Wagner became a world famous composer by sheer determination.

Wagner liked the theater, art, and music, but he disliked being on stage. He could draw nothing more complex than stick figures, and he was a slow learner on the piano. But his lack of talent was overcome by great determination.

He decided to become a composer at the age of 15. His prior musical training has been scanty, so he headed for the library, checked out a book on how to compose music, and committed every page to memory. To train his ear, he asked a violinist from the Leipzig Orchestra to teach him about chords and keys, learning the technique of every orchestral instrument but the harp. He studied the works of successful composers such as Beethoven to understand how to capture a sound.

Still, Wagner's early compositions were terrible. His first audience couldn't stop laughing. Embarrassed, the 17-year-old sneaked out of the theater.

To see what he had been doing wrong, Wagner sought the opinion of a local church musician. He was told to get a better understanding of the basics before setting out to try something new, so he began to go over the works of Bach and Mozart line by line until he began to understand how to construct a lyrical phrase.

Given a second chance, the audience liked his work and his career was on its way. Full of determination, Wagner once sat at the piano to write some music after lunch. Downstairs, a neighbor began to hammer on a sheet of tin, creating a terrible clamor. Instead of screaming at the neighbor or setting aside his music, he concentrated on the noise and began to make his music blend with the racket. That piece became part of a major scene in Wagner's famous opera *Siegfried*.

Bill Russell, whom many believe was the best defensive basketball player of all time has said he found many games to be so absorbing and intense that it made no difference to him who won or lost. He was consumed by determination to play his best.

Philip Knight, the founder of *NIKE* is convinced that the determination he needed to launch his business was far more rewarding than running a big company.

36. Look for a Better Way

One of the worst mistakes is to assume people are interchangeable and indistinguishable. People should expand their talents and abilities, and should become cross-trained in some instances, but they should not be put in a position that clearly does not leverage their best talents and potential.

Chester Carlson used the pain from arthritis in his hands to motivate him to develop a machine which Fortune Magazine once called "the most successful product in history."

Responsibility came early to young Chester. By age 14 he needed to work to support his invalid parents. His mother passed away when he was 17 and his father when he was 24. The early setbacks made him more determined. He put himself through Cal Tech, got a physics degree and was turned down by 82 firms before being hired by Bell Labs in New York. Laid off in 1933 he soon began experimenting with his ideas in the kitchen of his small apartment.

In 1934 Carlson's job was to make copies of drawings by hand. Day-after-day the pain got worse and he began to work on ways to replace carbon paper and mimeographs.

Finally in October 1938, Carlson and an associate, Otto Kornei, gave birth to the first office copier. His invention was turned down by 20 companies, including General Electric, RCA and IBM before being purchased in 1946 by Haloid, which added Xerox to its name in 1958.

37. Eliminate Obstacles

Most progress is stopped because we stop it. Not intentionally, but because we allow it by not learning how to eliminate obstacles. Erma Bombeck, the beloved humorist and author (1927-1996) was a great example. She started writing for her Junior High School paper and had a part time writing job at the *Dayton Ohio Journal-Herald* at age 15. Her job was to do whatever no one else wanted to do.

Although frightened by public speaking after she became famous as a writer and author, she quickly caught on by featuring the material that got the biggest laughs. The secret she believed was to "not make the same mistake twice."

In the 1890s, inventor Arthur Pitney believed that some day stamps would not be the only way to pay postage. He made a metering device for bulk mailings and received a patent in 1902. But the U.S. Postal Service rejected it time after time for 11 years. Then Pitney met Walter Bowes who sold stamp-canceling machines to the Post Office. Bowes, an experienced businessman, had many good contacts in the postal service, and persuaded them to grant Pitney and Bowes exclusive rights to dispense postage. Congress approved in 1920. By blending their strengths, they removed obstacles which neither could have removed alone. Pitney Bowes is now a $4 billion worldwide company.

Leaders lead from the front.

38. Become Trustworthy

Internal Struggle

The struggle to be trustworthy never ends.
It is the indispensable element of personal relationships.
It is the requirement that makes laws work.
The challenge is to earn trust:

1. Even when we are not feeling our best.
2. Even when no one else will know about it.
3. Even when the other person does not seem totally deserving.
4. Even when there is no direct benefit for us.
5. Even when the other person has offended us.
6. Even when it is inconvenient.
7. Even when the other person is not appreciative.
8. Even when conditions aren't completely right.
9. Even when the situation/circumstance is relatively minor.
10. Even when there is no praise for our good deed.

The next time your trustworthiness is challenged (and it will be soon) think about this list and remember – there is no substitute for the joy you will feel when it is reconfirmed.

39. Learn to Benchmark

Ignoring facts won't make them go away.

Benchmarking provides a continuous way to analyze how your products, services and practices compare with the competition. There are two types of benchmarking: Results and Process. With results benchmarking, you evaluate the end results. With Process benchmarking, you focus on the practices used to produce the end result.

- **Determine whether you want to improve processes or get results.**
  Identify performance measures within each process. These include quality, quantity, time and cost factors. Activities do not necessarily improve results. The only way to know for sure is to measure results actually achieved.
- **Identify the best-in-class in your field.**
  If you really want to be the best, you have to be able to prove it. Good intentions without accomplishment are worthless.
- **Ask others to participate in your benchmarking study.**
  Invite them to share information. To gather the information, you can conduct one-on-one interviews, send out questionnaires, or visit them. One of your best investments is to spend time developing contacts that can provide specific up-to-date information on what the best people in your field are doing and how they are doing it.

- **Analyze the results.**

Based on your performance measures, compare where you stand. Be sure you know why. Ask customers. Relentlessly quiz them.

- **Develop and implement plan for action.**

Turn the resulting data into some plan of action that will upgrade your position. Borrow processes from the best-in-class and integrate them into your own.

Some jobs are more difficult to measure than others, but every one can be measured. Keep in mind, however, that little is likely to happen unless *specific accountability* is assigned for each step. Objectives tell how much progress needs to be made and where to concentrate, but only an action plan describes *who* will do *what* by *when.*

To allow mediocrity is to endorse it.

---

40. Always Know <u>Who</u> Will Do <u>What</u> by <u>When</u>

In setting up your action plan, you must designate: a) *who* is to conduct each step, b) *what* activity or equipment is needed, c) *when* checkpoints need to be met, and d) alternative courses of action available.

Properly done, a thoughtful action plan will provide important benefits:

1. Time management will improve because there is agreement on where to concentrate, low priority activities can be dropped or reassigned, and there will be fewer "false starts" or changes in direction.
2. Teamwork will improve because key players have a common game plan.
3. Errors will decrease.
4. There will be fewer excuses.

Without an action plan, goals are merely good intentions. Action plans pin down accountability, by addressing the following vital questions:

- Is the objective really worth accomplishing? Will it make a significant difference?
- Will completing it be cost-effective?
- Do I know the financial impact? Is it significant?
- Have the necessary steps toward implementation been determined? In the right sequence?
- Have the right people been informed? Involved?
- Are the deadlines realistic?
- Are the interim checkpoints acceptable?

**Only 2 things cause change –
a burning desire
or a burning discomfort.**

5

What Winners Do . . . and Don't Do

I had a rule that I wouldn't ask anyone to do anything that I hadn't done or wasn't prepared to do.

—Charles Beckwith, founder, U.S. Army Delta Force

---

41. Base Your Reputation on Accountability

Charisma may bring fame but trustworthiness comes only from accountability.

The most effective leaders are those who acknowledge that their job requires special accountabilities and don't shrink from them. They realize that:

- They must consider the *total* organization, not just its parts.
- They must anticipate changes as they are needed and make them before it is too late.
- They must initiate action when there is no pressure to do so.
- They must select and hire people who are smarter than they are.
- They must seek trustworthy advisors who are not on their payroll.
- They must maintain outside contacts to keep up to date.
- They must see that no gaps develop between the decision makers and those who do the work.
- They must keep cool when others lose control.
- They must always insist on rewarding performance over seniority, credentials, or personal ties.

42. Keep Reaching

**Life is 5% the cards you're dealt
and 95% how you play them.**

**—Bob Basten, Founder and CEO, Centerprise Advisors,
when he learned he had Lou Gehrig's disease**

Bob Basten learned early how to bring out his best. Orphaned at 16 he lived with relatives and earned a college scholarship. He was a good enough football player to spend a year with the Minnesota Vikings.

A real competitor, by age 33 he was head of American Express's Tax and Business Services. Then, by age 36 he had formed one of the nation's largest middle market accounting firms. When that failed in 1999, he started Centerprise Advisers now a $170 million company with more than 1,000 employees.

But that's just the beginning of the Bob Basten story. In June of 2002, he was diagnosed with amyotrophic lateral sclerosis (ALS) known commonly as Lou Gehrig's disease. It is always fatal, usually within 5 years.

But how has he reacted? First and foremost he doesn't feel sorry for himself. "Now," he says "I tend to tell people more how I feel and that I appreciate them. It works better to drop their guard and be comfortable with who you are."

43. Prepare to Lead

You can give people titles ... and privileges ... but you can't give them leadership.

It's also true that leadership is not constant. It ebbs and flows. It shrinks or grows. Leadership depends on action. You are a leader only as long as you are effective.

But some basic qualities can be identified:

- **Leaders are self-confident and assured.** If they are not sure about what must be done they are able to find out. They know what kind of help they will need and where to get it. This self-confidence inspires other people to follow. The leader's lack of confidence is contagious. Bravado, braggadocio are quickly sensed. A leader's lasting power stems from respect.
- **Leaders are decisive.** Because they know what has to be done they can keep people headed in the right direction.
- **Leaders know how to delegate.** Because they are confident and self-assured, leaders do not feel threatened when they delegate authority. They realize their power comes from what is accomplished, so they are eager to do whatever they can to help others accomplish as much as possible.
- **Leaders know how to motivate.** To get the most out of people, they must be motivated. They must *want* to do their work, and the incentive of a paycheck often is not enough to bring out a worker's best efforts.
- **Leaders know the value of teamwork.** A leader knows that two can accomplish more than one, and that three can accomplish more than two. So they form teams of people who possess the right combinations of skills to get the job done.
- **Leaders monitor progress.** Having assigned the work, delegated the authority, and provided the necessary people, equipment, material and funds to get the job done, leaders make it a point not to interfere. They may step in to help out in a crisis, but they let their people do their work.

44. Keep Skills Current

Being prepared is absolutely essential to success. There's little doubt about that. But how can you tell if you are *truly* ready to handle the task? See what kind of answers you give to the following questions:

Am I "Good to Go?"

1. Be the supporter your spouse expects?
2. Be the example your children seek?
3. Be as self-disciplined as your parents want?
4. Be as steady as your brothers/sisters hope for?
5. Be as understanding as your friends would like?
6. Be the employee that your boss needs?
7. Be as reliable as your job requires?
8. Be as conscientious as your career calls for?
9. Be as forgiving as you know you should?
10. Be as respected as your integrity demands?

Where were you the strongest in answering those questions? Where were you the weakest? What is the evidence? What help is needed? Who could help? When will you ask for that help?

Those who are prepared are the most prompt, trustworthy, reliable, predictable, accurate, and respected. They are the best leaders because they are most likely to succeed.

45. Learn to Say <u>No</u>

When and how to say no is an absolute requirement for leaders. The first questions to be answered are:

- Is the issue involved a priority for us?
- Do facts support it?
- Is this person best qualified to go forward?
- Are resources available?
- Can the costs be justified?

Don't take on a burden of guilt when it's necessary to say *no* to someone. When you overextend, it can be interpreted as an invitation to ask for even more. Saying *yes* repeatedly without some return response makes you the victim. We must recognize that sometimes our ability to bring out our best will not be appreciated. Example: A photographer was invited to dinner with friends and took along a few photos to show the hostess. "These are very good!" she exclaimed. "You must have a good camera." At the end of the evening, the photographer thanked the hostess and said, "That was a really delicious meal! You must have very good pots."

46. Test Your Experience

**Without change, experience
can become a prison.**

It's not easy to bounce back after suffering a serious reversal, but it is possible to turn failure into a valuable experience. It's up to you. Will you:

1. **Adapt to reality?** This means refocusing the situation based on hard facts.
2. **Avoid revenge?** Don't play a continual soap opera of grief and anger for every passing ear.
3. **Mope?** Don't get stuck in self-pity, recrimination, and replaying the past.
4. **Pay your dues?** Create elaborate schemes, alibis, defenses, and explanations for your past and current failures. Move on.
5. **Enlist advocates on your side?** You usually won't do a good job of selling yourself or your case on its merits when you're emotional. Find someone willing and able to speak for you.
6. **Prepare alternatives?** Write down as many plausible options as you can. Don't let yourself get locked into a single one too soon.
7. **Define objectives?** Establish long-term objectives first. Then work up a checklist of immediate short-term objectives which will carry your plan to completion. You also should prepare a contingency plan in case the first choice doesn't work out.
8. **Commit to action?** Don't wait for something miraculous to happen.
9. **Persevere?** F.W. Woolworth went broke about nine times before he devised the merchandising strategy that made him rich. Abraham Lincoln lost every election he ran in . . . except one, for the Presidency. Tom Watson was fired from National Cash Register, so he

bounced back and picked up a small company called CTR (he renamed it IBM).

10. **Set tough, realistic, and attainable goals for yourself?** It's better to know yourself, like yourself, and be yourself than it is to waste your time, effort and energy in pursuit of perfection.

47. Meet Commitments

Losers usually think of themselves as victims. Winners never do.

A few things come easy. Most don't.

Baseball star Tony Gwynn of the San Diego Padres believes in proving yourself and doing what you say you will do. He learned this lesson from his parents, by "watching them work hard." When he first broke into baseball, he went to the minor leagues with the mentality that he was going to have to work hard to get into the big leagues.

His commitment to being honest with himself about his strengths and weaknesses really paid off. During his career, Tony won eight batting titles, tying him for the second most ever received in the big leagues. He had more than 3,100 hits and a career batting average of .338. He also won the Golden Glove award five times.

Gwynn retired as a player... and started a new career as a teacher. He has been the head baseball coach at San Diego State since July 2001.

Bobby Unser began racing cars at age 15. A few years later, he wanted to enter the famous Pike's Peak Climb. He couldn't afford to buy the official Firestone tires required so he experimented with recapped tires, which were ruled unsafe. Undaunted, Unser called the Goodyear Tire Company and was referred to a man in the development department who promptly said, "We'll make the tires you need." The company's willingness to have low-ranking people make important decisions impressed Unser so much, he stayed with Goodyear as a sponsor even when offered a million dollars to drive for another company.

48. Keep Options Open

Brilliance is a 2-edged sword:

1. Discovering what will work
2. Realizing what won't

We move forward or fall back one decision at a time. Here are a few examples which had gigantic consequences:

- In 1899 the owners of Coca Cola sold their bottling rights for $1.00 because they thought their product would only be sold at soda fountains.
- The founders of Apple Computers refused to license their McIntosh Operating System to other manufacturers. Result: Microsoft did license its Windows System and has dominated the market ever since.
- Henry Ford was eager to build small ships for the U.S. Navy in World War I. He said he could build *1,000 a*

day but encountered huge problems and produced only 17 in the first year!

The highest achievers are working so hard they quickly put failure behind them.

---

49. Expect Criticism

Ask yourself this question: "Have I learned more from criticism or compliments?" Usually it will be how we handle criticism that matters most. Frequently there is something good to be learned, from even the worst kind of situation. For example:

- **Having a demanding boss** can serve as a means of pushing you out of your 'comfort zone' and helping you to achieve things you didn't think possible.
- **If someone seems distant** you can take it as a signal that you need to know that individual better. We often assume that certain bonds just naturally develop between people who have worked together and that's not necessarily true. Don't take them for granted. Try to make each person feel they are the most important one in your life at that moment.
- **When something unfortunate occurs** dismiss it as quickly as possible. When you make a mistake, offend someone, over-react, or overlook something obvious, take responsibility for the oversight and move on. The question is not whether you will make a mistake, it's how quickly you will recover when you do.

- **Don't give in to your critics.** The more you achieve, the more criticism you will encounter. Don't let it bother you. A politician may win an election by taking 65 percent of the vote . . . but still must contend with the criticism of the 35 percent who wish he'd lost.

The best advice is to learn to listen. Ask for clarification. Get specific examples or instances from critics. Analyze each one objectively. Focus only on the ones which are justified.

Anne Morrow Lindbergh was thrust into the limelight immediately when she married the famous aviator Charles Lindbergh. But her dream was to be a writer and her method was self-discipline. She created time to write each day at the same time.

She too became a pilot, but wherever she traveled throughout the world, she found a space, pencil and paper to record her thoughts. She always *sought criticism* and input from experts and editors and became famous for her work.

50. Listen for Opportunity Clues

**Big shots are only little shots
who keep shooting.**

—Christopher Morley, writer

Harland Sanders, founder of Kentucky Fried Chicken, had tremendous obstacles to overcome. His father died when he was just six years old. When his mother went to work to support the family, he was left in charge of two younger children. He was forced to drop out of school. That's when he learned how to cook.

At age 10, Sanders got a job to help support the family. At one time or another, he worked as a farm hand, streetcar conductor, soldier, railroad firemen, and insurance agent. He didn't like any of those jobs. What he did like was fried chicken . . . and he knew that a lot of other people did too.

For a while, young Sanders cooked chicken and sold it at the gas station where he worked. Unfortunately, it took much too long so he began to look for some way to do it faster. He tried frying the chicken in a pressure cooker, but that didn't work the first time, so he tried again. And again. And again. He adjusted the cooking time, then the pressure, and then his recipe of spices until he had the best chicken he had ever tasted.

In 1952, Sanders started traveling the country by car. He would go from restaurant to restaurant, cooking samples of his chicken for the owner. If the owner liked it, he agreed to hand over the recipe and the method for cooking it in return for a franchise fee of five cents for each piece sold. A handshake sealed the deal.

Sanders' chicken became so popular the Governor of Kentucky made him and honorary colonel. His KFC franchises grew into a fast-food empire that had outlets in 82 countries and served more than two billion meals per year.

The key to this tremendous success – Colonel Sanders never gave up!

Work is the master key that opens
the door to all opportunities.

—Kemmons Wilson, Founder, Holiday Inn

6

Divided We Fall

**The cemeteries are full
of indispensable people.**
—Charles de Gaulle, Prime Minister of France

---

51. Form a Winning Team

**If I understand you, you are more likely
to understand me.**

The only way to multiply your own efforts effectively is to build a winning team. The worst mistake most people make when they see this need is to involve others like them. Soon they are top heavy with too many of the same types.

The key is to select people whose talents, experiences and interests supplement and complement each other. Only then can a group tap into a broader perspective on any given problem or situation.

Samuel F. B. Morse spent years developing his ideas for an electric telegraph in the 1830s but nothing happened. It wasn't until he gathered a team of associates – a politician, a businessman and a scientist – that he could lobby Congress to build a telegraph line from Washington to Baltimore. Ten years later he got the money. Few thought it would work, but use during the Civil War made everyone a believer.

Joan Ganz Cooney, originator of TV's *Sesame Street* believes in encouraging people to challenge her when they think they have a better idea. "I liked being told I was wrong and was saved from many errors by people who argued with me and made their case," she says. *Sesame Street* has won more Emmys than any show in the history of television (86).

52. Help Your Team Do Better

Teams work best when their leader shows confidence in them. As Robert Townsend, former president of Avis Rent-A-Car put it, "Leaders must have the discipline not to keep pulling up the flowers to see if their roots are healthy."

To truly spotlight teamwork and stop putting out fires, bring people into the loop and look beyond the obvious. Uninformed people will be less productive and more critical. Here are four ways to address both problems.

- **Share financial figures and performance results.** Don't gloss over problems. Explain what the facts mean. By sharing information, you can not only quell rumors, but give people what they need to improve.
- **Expand the circle.** Explain who does what and why. It will help people make better decisions and build a collective sense of teamwork.
- **Don't hide the bad news.** Decision-making need not – and should not – be a closed-door process.
- **Favor Problem Solvers.** Managers who can't resolve conflicts and co-workers who cause them are among the main reasons for employee back-stabbing. When hiring, ask the candidate questions, such as:

What do you do when you can't get along with a co-worker or boss?

Who's the most difficult person you've ever worked with? Why?

Remember, the best people respond to treatment which they believe will bring out their best.

53. Confront Conflicts

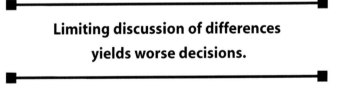

Limiting discussion of differences yields worse decisions.

Conflict is inevitable, but it doesn't have to be bad. It all depends on the behavior of those who have to deal with it. Constructive action helps to resolve conflict quicker vs. inflaming the situation and making it last longer.

Consider these four areas of constructive action.

- **Actively listen before response.** Actively listen to other people and show that you genuinely want to understand their points of view. Look at them while they are talking. Ask questions. In your own words, restate, giving them a chance to clarify what they're saying. Wait to give your own opinions, and after you have done so, ask for feedback. Rather than trying to "win" as if you were in some sort of a contest, honestly try to find out why they feel the way they do.

- **Focus on solutions.** Strive to focus on the problem and not on the people involved. Try to get at the root causes. Winners examine root causes. Losers look only at surface symptoms. Avoid "sore points" that encourage greater confrontation. Look for points of mutual agreement and work on those points first; then go on to the points of difference. Brainstorm possible solutions.

- **Give reasons without emotion.** Speak honestly about your feelings. Tell *why* you feel the way you do. Speak up, and be honest, but in a thoughtful, controlled manner.

Talk to me and I'll listen.
Scream and I become deaf.

- **Offer new options.** Take the first step toward compromise. Discuss past mistakes and how the issue might have been handled differently. If you learn that you did something to hurt someone, apologize.

54. Take Responsibility

Without responsibility, all action is tentative, all progress doubtful.

In 1970, Frank Robinson, the Hall of Fame baseball player, was appearing in a game against the Boston Red Sox. Robinson hit a ball that he thought would be a home run, so he left the batter's box at a leisurely home run trot. Unfortunately, the ball failed to clear Fenway Park's 37-foot left field wall, Sox left fielder Carl Yastrzemski played the rebound perfectly, and Robinson was held to a single when he could easily have made it to second or even third.

The team had a big lead, so the play had no impact on the game's outcome, but after the game was over, Robinson put a $100 bill and a note on the manager's desk. The note said: "I embarrassed baseball. I embarrassed the team. I embarrassed all of my teammates. I embarrassed you, and most of all, I embarrassed myself. It's never going to happen again."

Frank Robinson was the National League Rookie of the Year in 1956, tying the rookie season record with 38 home runs. His 586 career home runs rank fourth in the major leagues. He is the only player in major league history to be named Most Valuable Player in both leagues, the National

League in 1961 and the American League in 1966. He was elected to the Baseball Hall of Fame in 1982.

Following his playing days, Robinson became the major leagues' first black manager, joining the Cleveland Indians in 1975. He managed in the majors for eight full seasons and for parts of three others. He was named American League Manager of the Year in 1989 with the Baltimore Orioles. He later became Major League Baseball's vice president of on-field operations.

Many military experts believe that Brigadier General John Buford's sense of responsibility was the turning point in the Civil War. Instead of retreating at the sight of General Robert E. Lee's Army near Gettysburg, Pennsylvania, Buford determined he must delay it long enough for Union forces to take the high ground at the Gettysburg Battlefields. After fighting all night on June 30, 1863, his 1,500 men still faced 10,000 confederates. They had kept Lee's entire army at bay for 4 hours so that Union forces were positioned to win at Gettysburg on July 2 & 3.

55. Get Close to the Action

The most effective people are close to the action. They don't try to deal with problems from afar. They get out and "go where the action is." This is most important when dealing directly with customers. Ronald Sargent, CEO of Staples, Inc., will stop in unannounced at company stores. If he finds one that's not what it should be, he quickly initiates corrective action.

Problems get worse when we have to guess about the real reasons for them. The solutions depend upon:

- **approachability** – being available to listen, advise and assist when needed
- **continuous training** to provide needed skills and remove obstacles
- **sharing information** needed before and emergency develops
- **meeting one-on-one** to bring problems to the surface
- **rewarding results** when they happen rather than on a set schedule. Delayed recognition loses its impact
- **personalizing awards and recognition** – Don't assume that everyone is motivated by the same thing.

56. Identify Accountable People

Most business failure is caused not by lack of money but because of discovering too late that the wrong people have been involved.

The following profile was developed

The *Least Valuable People* (LVP) Profile

~~I developed this profile~~ as a means of identifying the individuals who are now behaving in a way which will likely cause them to fail. ~~Note that~~ only 2 answers are allocated to each issue: Guilty (G) and Not Guilty (N).

Start by rating yourself first.

Name: _____

1. Constantly sidesteps problems and complaints, hoping someone else will handle them.   ☐G☐N

2. Avoids disciplining people.   ☐G☐N

3. Blames others when things go wrong.   ☐G☐N

4. Allows false statements to go unchallenged.   ☐G☐N

5. Doesn't worry about being late for work or meetings.   ☐G☐N

6. Postpones completion of projects as long as possible.   ☐G☐N

7. Avoids seeking clarification of misunderstandings in order to criticize later.   ☐G☐N

8. Never volunteers for an assignment when not absolutely certain of success.   ☐G☐N

9. Doesn't worry about deadlines.   ☐G☐N

10. Maintains the same sources of information and bases decisions more on opinions than facts.   ☐G☐N

11. Tries to be as noncommittal as possible.   ☐G☐N

12. Punishes good people who disagree.   ☐G☐N

13. Sees delegating as a way of getting rid of unpleasant chores rather than improving and expanding productivity.   ☐G☐N

14. Keeps busy on current projects and is uncomfortable about future planning.   ☐G☐N

15. Allows someone else to do recruiting and selection.   ☐G☐N

16. Tends to criticize others in public, rather than in private.   ☐G☐N

17. Is insulated from contact with   □G□N
    customers.
18. Frequently talks about how much others □G□N
    depend on them.
19. Is not concerned about nurturing   □G□N
    promotable people.
20. Is uncomfortable when depending on   □G□N
    others to provide answers.
21. Concentrates efforts on favorite tasks □G□N
    rather than highest priorities.
22. Rarely compliments others for their   □G□N
    good work.
23. Downplays the competence of other   □G□N
    people.
24. Takes as few risks as possible.   □G□N
25. Waits as long as possible before   □G□N
    delivering bad news.
26. Limits efforts to "on-the-job" hours; □G□N
    rarely takes work home.
27. Is not involved in self-improvement   □G□N
    programs.
28. Joins in conversations about the "good □G□N
    old days" as often as possible.
29. Talks a lot about how difficult it is to □G□N
    objectively measure what they do.
30. Hides talented people to further their □G□N
    own career.

Now take the opportunity to analyze the results of your study, as follows:

0-4 Guilty verdicts: This is the accountable person you need most. Don't let them get away.

5-10 Guilty verdicts: This person is likely to qualify for greater responsibility with proper coaching and management.

11-20 Guilty verdicts: This person is making you more vulnerable every day – watch them carefully.

More than 20 Guilty verdicts: This person is likely to seriously handicap you. Don't wait too long to release them.

57. Get the Help You Need

Keep away from people who try to belittle your ambitions. Small people always do that, but the really great make you feel that you, too, can become great.

—Mark Twain

Successful people acknowledge that they are vulnerable in their dependence upon the performance of others. They also realize they can *benefit* by selecting people who will enhance their own capabilities.

Using the LVP profile, you can learn to avoid problem situations before they get worse. You can ask people to rate themselves then discuss how their answers compare with yours. This will put the spotlight on several of the key requirements needed to make your relationship succeed. It will also help identify the potential of those who:

- **Go above and beyond expectations.** They don't stop when they've achieved what others have done before them.
- **Bring solutions, not more problems.** Their track record indicates that they never say: "You have a problem," but rather: "*We* have a problem. Let me see if I can give you some recommendations to solve it."
- **Bounce back from mistakes.** They do not blame others for their own errors. They rarely say, "I did what you told me and it was wrong." They are resilient and find new ways to do things.
- **Don't make excuses.** If things go wrong, they admit and go on to fix the problem.
- **Don't depend on reminders to complete their work.** They are able to set interim deadlines for long-range tasks so they don't panic on the due date.
- **Work for improvement, not perfection.** People who seek perfection in everything they do tend to get frustrated and put themselves under so much pressure that they rarely accomplish what they are capable of doing.
- **Think ahead.** This helps to eliminate unpleasant surprises.
- **Don't dwell on successes.** They quickly move on from past accomplishments as well as past mistakes.
- **Don't assume too much.** When in doubt, they ask for clarification.
- **Negotiate agreements and then get going.** They don't wait for orders to be sure they are doing everything *exactly* as it was before.

The people most needed are initiators, negotiators and teachers/trainers. If you are finding, hiring and keeping people who are strong in those ten areas, your chances of success are great.

58. Share the Spotlight

Loyalty is not a one-way proposition. It is mutual and must be learned. Here are the starting points:

- **Start off positively.** Get as much agreement as possible at the beginning and *then* move on to the thornier issues.
- **Solicit ideas.** Draft an outline of your thoughts and give it to your team (or a committee) for their critique and refinement. Your idea can now become theirs. The key: Make sure the team gets full credit for the result. Check up with progress reports.
- **Let others add refinements.** Don't discount any ideas. Let them build on each other.
- **Offer incentives.** Provide rewards for the ideas with the best payoff. Allow potential recipients to determine what rewards they value most. Don't decide by yourself.

Jack Taylor understood these incentives very well when he started his car rental business in 1957. He began by giving those he hired authority to deal directly with customers in meeting their needs and providing a very progressive profit sharing plan. Enterprise Rent-A-Car now has 50,000 employees and a fleet of 500,000 vehicles. In 2002, revenues exceeded $6.5 billion. It is the largest car rental company in North America.

59. Avoid Manipulative People

To avoid trouble, never introduce enemies to those you aren't sure of.

Difficult people come in all forms and styles, from screamers to schemers. The key is to remember that difficult people aren't reacting to you personally. Their focus is usually on themselves.

You may not be able to change difficult personalities, but with a little planning you can help to ensure a positive outcome from a negative situation. Here are some suggestions:

- If you feel that someone is trying to manipulate you, be polite but not overfriendly. If you distance yourself from manipulative people, you lessen their hold on you.
- Liars are the ultimate manipulators, seeking not only to manipulate you but to manipulate truth as well. When confronting dishonest people, steer clear of personalities and stick to the facts. Let the truth expose both the liar and the lie. Don't be too eager to pass judgment by yourself; rather, let others also see the truth.

- When gathering support for an idea or project, make sure the support is solid. Get agreement to have supporters' names included on a well-circulated memo outlining the project and its goals. When the blame or credit is shared, everyone will work harder to ensure the project's success.
- Try to bring the critics into your camp with a comment like "I know you've got strong opinions on this, so I thought it would be best to discuss the project in detail so I could get your perspective early on."
- When dealing with people who say one thing but later claim to have meant something else, repeat their words back to them and assure mutual understanding. Getting a person to confirm what they said will make denial a lot less likely down the road.

60. Watch for Little Things

Show me a man who cannot bother to do little things and I'll show you a man who cannot be trusted to do big things.

—Lawrence Bell, aviation executive

Long-term benefits require daily attention to the little things. Added up, they determine whether people will give their best efforts, day in and day out. They are the deciding factor enabling you to keep your best people and to attract the new ones you want and need.

How well do you handle the little things? Evaluate yourself by answering these questions:

1. **Do I acknowledge accomplishments as they happen?** Don't wait until the time seems right to you; do it when the time seems right for them.
2. **Do I show personal interest in what people are doing?** Find out what personal services people are providing for customers. Ask yourself: "I need Sam or Mary because . . ." If you are not sure, it will show in your attitude toward them. They must know that you appreciate them.
3. **Do I play favorites?** If the same people are continuously acknowledged and others are not, awards will lose their value. The remedy is to look for people doing good work who have not been acknowledged recently.
4. **Have I deceived myself into thinking that because I am a thoughtful person, other I select will be too?** Never assume. Keep an eye on the people you choose for key jobs to ensure they are as thoughtful and caring as you want them to be. Don't let uncaring people stay too long.
5. **Do I remember the people who work behind the scenes?** They may not be readily visible to you on a daily basis but they are usually very important to your customers and suppliers. All too often, people get the impression that only high-ranking jobs are important.
6. **Do I praise in public and criticize in private?** This is a good motto, but much can be gained by private acts of gratitude as well. For example: One company president provided transportation for a sick family member. The loyalty gained from such acts simply cannot be measured in monetary terms.

7. **Do I create new ways to say "Thank You?"** In addition to verbal praise, provide some tangible token of appreciation – a letter from a satisfied customer, a small gift everyone can share, or a symbol of employees' accomplishments that everyone can see and pass around. Mention the achievement in public to as many people as you can, as frequently as you can. Don't be vague: Give the names of those who deserve the credit. Above all, be sure to include those who did the actual work.

8. **Do I take people for granted?** If you want people to know they are appreciated, you must convincingly and continuously show them. After all, they know you couldn't do it without their help.

Education is when you read the fine print.
Experience is what you get if you don't.

—Pete Seeger, singer and songwriter

7

Performance Pays

> There are two ways to get to the top
> of an oak tree. Sit on an acorn and wait
> for it to grow or climb it.
> —**Bill Rosenberg, Founder of Dunkin' Donuts**

61. Get Up and Get Going

> **Optimists change and prosper.**
> **Pessimists stay put and fade.**

Successful people concentrate on 5 basics and practice them regularly.

They are: 1) preparation, 2) belief in yourself, 3) active listening, 4) learning from mistakes, and 5) using stress to your advantage. None are inherited. Each must be learned, then applied regularly and consistently in order to be effective.

Whenever obstacles stop progress, it's time for a serious internal evaluation of fundamentals. Too often, we look for a scapegoat – a condition, an individual, or a circumstance to blame. This never corrects the problem or prevents it from recurring.

Looking for scapegoats makes your own inadequacies even more obvious by indicating that you do not have the situation under control. Instead, try to see if you can uncover any hidden weaknesses. Ask yourself:

- Am I shooting for an unrealistic goal?
- Was my goal the right one?
- Did I communicate requirements to everyone who needs to know?
- Have I misinterpreted signals from people I need to help me?
- Have the right assignments be given to the right people, with the right resources, and the right authority to do the work?
- Do I use my own time wisely?
- Do I provide appropriate incentives for individuals and groups?

These self-assessment questions are *always* important, not just after a serious crisis has occurred. If a periodic tuneup is vital for your car, it is no less important for your career. Ask yourself:

- Am I facing the same problems over and over again?
- Are good people leaving?
- Do good people feel they are too restricted?
- Do relationships seem more strained than in the past?
- Do I spend enough time with the people whose support I need?
- Are there "problem" people who should be replaced?

Even if you have only one or two *yes* or *not sure* answers, you should be concerned. If you have three or four, your situation is likely to get progressively worse.

When it's over, retreat.
When in doubt, stand still.
When certain, move forward now.'

---

62. Practice, Practice, Practice

Sure, baseball is a game. A game is supposed to be fun, not hard work. Don't tell that to anyone who earns his living playing baseball. He can tell you that baseball, like anything else, requires study, study, study . . . practice, practice, practice . . . and lots of hard work.

Johnny Bench was only 19 years old when he was promoted to be catcher for the Cincinnati Reds. But even at that young age, Bench knew that the duties of a catcher were far more complex than the average fan might suppose. He realized he must know the batting tendencies of every player on every team his club must face. Does he bat left-handed or right-handed? Does he like a pitch that's high or low? A fast ball or a curve ball? Thrown inside or outside?

A catcher must also know the strengths and weaknesses of everyone on his own team. After a right-handed batter has moved away from the plate and a left-handed batter takes his place, should the infield change positions? The outfield?

As a young rookie, experienced veterans sometimes resented it when the teenager began giving them directions. But Bench held his ground. He believed that if he stopped to doubt himself or let a shortstop play where he didn't think he ought to, or made even the least little excuse for his age, he would be quickly demoted back to the minor leagues.

Bench brought out the best in the Reds' pitchers. He studied their strengths and matched them against opposing batters' weaknesses. He encouraged them . . . and set them straight when necessary.

Bench knew that it isn't wise to be smug. "Don't think you're as good as you (can be)," he says. "You can always be better . . . but you must be prepared every day."

- Practice paid off big time for Johnny Bench. He became the first catcher ever to win the Rookie of the Year award. In 1970, he was named the Most Valuable Player in the National League after his team won 102 games. He hit .293 and led both leagues with 45 home runs and 148 RBIs.
- In 1972, the Reds won their division, and Bench again won MVP honors as well as leading the majors in

home runs (40) and RBIs (125). With Bench behind the plate, the Reds won the World Series twice (1975 and 1976).
- He was elected to the Baseball Hall of Fame in 1989, and was named the starting catcher on Major League Baseball's All-Century Team in 1999.

63. Move Out of Your Comfort Zone

Losers resist changes that do not bring physical comfort.
Winners change before they must.

Nobody goes through life without a mistake. The key is to learn from them, pick yourself up, and move on. It's what you do afterward that counts.

These four attitudes are critical:

- **Stop kicking yourself.** Instead of getting upset, losing focus, or giving up after making a mistake, use the error as an opportunity to learn something about yourself.
- **Avoid negative thinking.** Don't let disappointment, anger, or frustration cloud your ability to analyze the problem. If you can stay in control of your emotions, you will be better prepared to find the solution or to figure out how to avoid the situation if it arises again.

Once you've controlled your reaction, you can clear your mind and start again.

- **Reflect on what you did right.** When mistakes are magnified and positive qualities are minimized, it's hard to maintain commitment or overcome new challenges.
- **Forget being perfect.** When you think you have to be perfect you set yourself up for disappointment and frustration. It is much more difficult to move past failures and locate the positives after a mistake occurs if you try to demand perfection of yourself.

To illustrate – have you heard about the time Saint Peter and God decided to play a round of golf? On the first tee, God won the coin-toss and hit a drive that traveled 450 yards. The drive went a little off-line and the ball hit a tree beside the green. Bouncing off the tree, it headed for a neighboring pond, but as the ball dropped toward the pond, a turtle surfaced. The ball hit the turtle on the back, bounced into the air, and landed on the green 40 feet from the pin. The ball was running straight toward a sand trap when a raven suddenly swept out of the sky, grabbed the ball and began to fly off with it. Out of a cloudless sky, a bolt of lightning struck the raven, which dropped the ball ... straight into the cup.

Back on the tee, Saint Peter turned to God and calmly inquired, "Are we gonna play golf or fool around?"

64. Measure Yourself

**The best Performers have a built-in urge
to measure and be measured.**

Fortunately, Orel Hershiser learned early in life to be
his own best critic. He was twice cut from his high school
baseball team. He received lots of criticism from his early
coaches. But he learned to persevere. The keys?

- He developed a sense of discipline early, including
  grueling daily workouts that sometimes ran to three
  and one-half hours long. He engaged in weightlift-
  ing, abdominal and shoulder exercises, and hour-long
  cardiovascular workouts.
- He wasn't willing to let those results . . . good or bad . . .
  change his intensity, concentration, or preparation
  for the next game.
- Self-examination was always important. He inven-
  toried his skills, in good times and bad. He analyzed
  his performances in video replays. "I could actually
  watch what I was doing as if I were someone else
  watching me do it," he says.

The results? Hershiser played for four major league
teams throughout his career: the Los Angeles Dodgers,
Cleveland Indians, San Francisco Giants, and New York
Mets. He won the Cy Young Award and the National League

Golden Glove Award. In 1988, he broke Don Drysdale's record, pitching 59 consecutive scoreless innings and remarkably, was able to pitch in the major leagues until he was in his early 40s.

65. Don't Bluff

The truth will ultimately prevail over messages which are "spun."

The least effective (and most dangerous) people in leadership positions are pretenders. They want you to believe they know what they are doing and will do anything to get you to trust them or vote for them.

Alan Bean (now 70) was one of thousands of applicants to become an astronaut. He didn't make the final list of 35 chosen but he would not pout. He decided it was up to him to do everything he could to be on the list the next time. He read every book he could find on space flight. He worked out daily to stay in top physical shape. He had a positive attitude about every assignment.

Says Bean, "Even if you are not naturally the most gifted person, if you will work harder at it, study and do your homework, you can move real close to the person who is."

Former Chrysler CEO Lee Iacocca summed it up well: "In the end, your legacy is: Did you know what you were doing? Were you building good products, were you giving good advice, were you giving good service, and were your employees happy doing it?"

66. Nurture Achievers

About the meanest thing you can say about a man is that he means well.

—Harry Truman, 33rd U.S. President

Unless they are understood and coached, some *achievers* can create problems for themselves as well as for an organization. They need:

- **Assignments** that not only challenge their capabilities and drive, but also offer training for skills essential for future advancement. Warren Buffet, the second wealthiest man in the country, says, "Too many times, the boss shoots the arrow of managerial performance and then hastily paints the bull's-eye around the spot where it lands."
- **Testing** in terms of how quickly they adjust strategies to seize an opportunity or solve a problem – how effectively they make critical decisions.
- **Recognition** for work well done.
- **Evaluation** to 1) see how well they respond under pressure and 2) how people respond to them and their ideas.

67. Deal with Problem People

**Rudeness is the weak man's
imitation of strength.**

—Eric Hoffer, philosopher

On the other end of the spectrum, you must also learn to deal with those who cause problems, or worse yet, *are* themselves the problem. How do you turn difficult people into productive ones?

Analysis involves much more than defining a single problem or incident. Often, it requires tracing a behavior pattern over a period of time using these sources:

- **Current levels of performance.** Is the person co-operative? Dependable? Willing to do their share? Reasonably skilled? Most of all, what *results* have been achieved?
- **Physical and mental health factors**. Under what circumstances do they lose their temper? Talk with them. Get a feel for their communication skills, personal aspirations and goals, outside interests, and family life.
- **Career blockers.** Observe the support and cooperation they receive from others. Who withholds support, and why? Determine the degree of personal initiative. Do they take pride in their work? Do they have high self-esteem?

Finally, analyze information you have gathered to reveal the severity of any personal barriers that may exist between you and them. As you pull the facts together and consider possible courses of action, remember these essential steps:

- **Ask questions.** What condition may have caused their problem? When? Where? With what frequency? Are the facts you have collected conclusive?
- **Arrange your facts.** Organize them in order of their importance so you focus your time and attention on essential matters. Do the facts suggest the need for a new approach?
- **Jot down the possibilities.** Should others be involved? If so, who? Is marked improvement possible? What would be the cost in time and money?
- **Outline a course of action.** List your options and select the one most likely to resolve the problem, or at least bring it under control. Detail who must do what . . . and by when.

68. Follow-Through

Noah Webster's name is known by everyone who has used his American Dictionary of the English Language. What most *don't* know is that:

- He spent 20 years researching and writing it.
- To be accurate, he learned 26 languages, including Arabic, Hebrew and Sanskrit.

- After completion in 1828 he spent many more years going from town to town with his horse and buggy trying to convince printers to produce it and schoolmasters to sell it.

His persistence and follow-through resulted in his dictionary becoming second only to the Bible as the best selling book of all time (over 55 million copies). His legacy is a deep and lasting impression on American culture.

69. Be Decisive

When I've heard all I need to make a decision, I don't take a vote. I make a decision.

—Ronald Reagan, 40th U.S. President

Avoiding decisions invites disaster. Too many people think of decision making in the same category as a lottery, a guess or a chance. They are wrong. Those who make the best decisions prepare thoroughly and systematically.

Hector Boiardi left his home in Italy for America at age 17. He had worked in a variety of restaurants observing chefs since he was 11. In New York City, he worked at both the Plaza and Ritz Carlton hotels, where he again spent as much time as possible quizzing and watching the chefs.

By the time he moved to Cleveland in the 1930s, he had decided to combine his own spaghetti sauce with packets of dry pasta and cheese and sell it to take-out customers.

He put his Americanized name, *Boyardee*, on the product, which became one of the first ever pre-packaged meals. The brand remains popular to this day.

70. Motivate Yourself

**Success requires mining the gold
in your own mind.**

The common denominator for almost all successful inventors/creators is self-motivation. Consider these examples from ordinary people who have influenced our everyday lives:

- In 1929 Charles Branock, son of a shoe store owner, spent his college years developing a device for measuring shoe size. Since then, sales have exceeded 1 million units.
- In 1935 Carl Magee, a member of the Oklahoma City Chamber of Commerce Traffic Committee, invented the first parking meter.
- In 1936 Henry Phillips patented the now indispensable recessed-cross screw design bearing his name. Assembly line workers plagued by daily problems with slot screws were overjoyed.
- In 1937 grocery store owner Sylvan Goldman crossed two wire baskets with a folding chair on wheels. His shopping carts made him a millionaire.

- In 1949 Robert Abplanalp, age 27, a machine operator in the Bronx, devised a cheap, reliable, mass-producible valve for aerosol cans. He collected 300 patents for cans used an estimated 1 billion times a day.
- In 1982 researcher Sam Hurst developed an overlay of conductive sheets that became the first touch screen for television. It is now an $800 million market.
- In 2000 Sara Blakely began production of her control-top panty hose. Sales jumped to $400,000 in the first four months.

Few people realize that Alexander Graham Bell's invention of the telephone was not a matter of chance. In fact, competition to develop a telephone was quite intense and Bell knew that he would have to compete against such noted inventors as Thomas Edison and Elisha Gray, among others. Virtually all of his competition had large staffs at their disposal, while Bell and his partner Thomas Watson had only each other to rely upon.

When Bell complained to Joseph Henry, secretary of the Smithsonian Institution, that he lacked the necessary understanding of electricity to build the telephone, Henry simply replied, "Get it!" Bell filed for his patent on February 14, 1876. Gray filed an application just two hours later! "There are no unsuccessful experiments," said Bell. "If we stop... it is *we* who are unsuccessful, not the experiments."

**Few good things are accidental,
most are caused by will power.**

8

Find a New Way

Be prepared to resign.
It will improve your value ...
and does wonders for your performance.
—Donald Rumsfeld, Secretary of Defense

---

71. Stretch Your Imagination

Very few starters of successful businesses are brilliant inventors or scientists. Success usually comes to those who produce a common product or perform a common service ... but do it faster, better, or less expensively than their competition. They stretch their imagination. That's what happened to Peter Hodgson.

When World War II began, it became apparent that the United States was in dire need of a substitute for rubber. Our sources were in the Far East, a region suddenly under enemy control. Research laboratories across the country quickly began to investigate the possibility of producing a synthetic rubber. One company, General Electric, created an unusual substance that they called "gupp."

Gupp could stretch further than rubber, be shaped under pressure, and bounce against a hard surface better than rubber. There was one insurmountable problem. It would slowly settle back into a shapeless, useless "puddle."

Still, gupp had enough qualities to make it fascinating . . . and fun. It was absolutely harmless, therefore not dangerous if it came into contact with the skin or eyes . . . or even if ingested. Pressed against a sheet of newspaper, it would pick up the print, either black-and-white or color.

Hodgson first saw gupp at a party where people were laughing at, and exploring its unusual properties. An unemployed ex-copywriter $12,000 in debt, Hodgson considered marketing the product for its entertainment qualities. He borrowed $147, bought 21 pounds of gupp, and convinced a guest at the party, a woman who owned a toy store, to put the item in her Christmas catalog. It outsold every other item except one – a box of Crayolas.

Hodgson believed in his discovery but the toy store owner did not and backed out. He decided to go on alone . . . and renamed his product Silly Putty.

Using the profits he'd made from the catalog sales, Hodgson ordered some plastic eggs and hired a few young people to stuff them with Silly Putty. He priced the eggs at $1 apiece, and headed for the International Toy Fair in New York City. Reception there was cold, but he persisted and finally persuaded Neiman Marcus and Doubleday Bookshops to carry it. In 1950, *The New Yorker* magazine featured it in the "talk of the Town" section. Hodgson received 250,000 orders in three days.

Concerned that Silly Putty would not endure in the adult market, he directed his marketing toward children ... and the newly-emerging medium of television. After being seen on shows like *Howdy Doody* and *Captain Kangaroo*, two of the most popular children's shows, it became a must-have children's toy.

When Hodgson died in 1976, he left an estate worth $140 million.

Never put a person with a cookie-cutter mentality in a position requiring creativity.

---

72. Wipe Out Waste

Continuous improvement requires constant emphasis on identifying, quantifying, and eliminating waste: waste of material, waste of capital, waste of time, waste of words, and waste from lost sales or missed opportunities.

Ken Iverson learned these lessons well. He took over Navcor in 1965 and build it into the #1 Steel Company in the U.S. with $4.6 billion in sales. Even then, with a workforce of over 8,000 people, Navcor's corporate headquarters had only 42 people located on 1 floor of a plain building in Charlotte, North Carolina. The no-frills approach enabled it to 1) have 140 successive quarters of profitability, 2) avoid layoffs, 3) pay employees 30-40% above the industry average and 4) have only 4 levels between the CEO and production workers.

All forms of work are subject to waste, whether the work is being done by people, machines, chemical processes, computers, or anything else.

Eliminating waste requires a detailed knowledge of the work itself – the kind of knowledge that is held by the people who are actually doing it. That is where almost all waste reduction must begin and end.

High quality at low cost is the only real employment security. All progress is not measured in miles. Sometimes an inch will do.

Here are the basic questions which must be answered to keep waste under control:

- Does each step add value?
- Is there duplication?
- Can we eliminate any delays?
- How much rework do we do?
- Is the sequence the most efficient possible?
- What can be combined?
- What should be eliminated?
- What can be simplified? To illustrate, "a recent government publication on the marketing of cabbage contains 26,941 words. The Gettysburg Address contains a mere 279 words while the Lord's Prayer comprises but 67."

73. Shrink Your Weaknesses

Weaknesses are what we allow them to be. Paul Orfalea flunked 2nd grade and was classified as a slow learner because he couldn't read or spell. Tests by specialists didn't help because not much was known about dyslexia in the mid 1950s.

Even with the help of tutors and special education classes things didn't change much and he graduated close to the bottom of his high school class. Undaunted, he took courses requiring little reading at a local community college and was eventually able to transfer to the University of Southern California.

A class at USC required research he could not do so he volunteered to do the legwork including all the photocopying at the University Library. There he saw his opportunity. He borrowed $5,000 and started a copy shop near the campus. His charge was 4¢ per page – less than ½ the going rate. Before long, Orfalea had stores near Universities all over the West Coast. By 2000, he had more than 1,000 outlets in 10 countries serving over 200,000 customers a day.

One night in November when I was 15 years old, I woke up with the worst pain in my back and left leg I have ever had. The diagnosis was polio. For a year or so, I was devastated. How could I ever be in sports again? How would I ever be able to compete in anything? But then I began to appreciate my assets. In every other way, my body was healthy and I could read, write, study and most of all *think*. It was then I made up my mind that if some people wanted to think of me as limited or handicapped, that was up to them. But as far as I am concerned, I can be competitive in any area I want to be.

Success only comes from effort.

—Joan Ganz Cooney, founder of TV's Sesame Street

74. Try Another Route

Insanity is continuing to do the same thing expecting different results.
—Albert Einstein, physicist

In 1968, a University of Michigan study divided 475 participants into two groups. Both groups were asked to find solutions to the same assembly-line scheduling problem. They were given identical instructions with one exception: The second group was told to "be creative." The result: 52% of people in the second group came up with what experts deemed "high-quality solutions," compared with 39% in the first group. Conclusion: *You get what you ask for.*

The best way to achieve an objective is to break it down into its component parts and solve them one by one. This makes it possible to try many options every step of the way. To get people to generate new ideas to find new ways, remember:

- Ask for input and advice from the people doing the "hands-on" work.
- Experimentation requires leadership by people who are dedicated to continuous improvement and who can act as coaches as well as players.
- Leaders remove barriers.

- Leaders are good listeners and communicators. They observe, study and question.
- Leaders show interest and appreciation, and they handle mistakes professionally.
- To achieve continuous improvement, organizations must recognize and reward those who find new and better ways.

75. Find Allies

When there is more work than one person can do and no authority to hire more people, the best approach is allies. Tom Sawyer found help to paint his fences because he was smart enough to 1) make the work attractive 2) make his ally feel needed and important. Simple skills, but *very* effective.

To keep allies involved and motivated, these ground-rules will help:

- Listen to and show respect for each other.
- Engage in problem solving as partners.
- Allow free expression and ideas.
- Provide frequent feedback – especially on controversial matters.
- Demonstrate a tolerance for conflicting viewpoints.

76. Take Time to Teach

People work more effectively when they 1) know what is expected and 2) have a stake in the outcome. Soliciting their ideas and showing them respect enhances their self-esteem – a powerful motivator.

The team concept is critical. Once people see that their help is really wanted, they feel a sense of "ownership" in solving a problem. Team members who are working toward continuous improvement are happy to contribute their brains and energy to the task, and they feel a sense of pride in their work.

Proper training is essential. Tools must be provided so people can apply their knowledge and skills.

Craig Tysdal is the CEO of NetSolve, a $46 million computer network management company in Austin, Texas. But he thinks of himself as Chief Teacher. For more than 5 years he has conducted a 3 part mandatory course on customer service for every new employee including those who will have no direct contact with customers. So far 275 people have taken his "course."

Tysdal say he doesn't delegate his teaching to anyone else because "the attitude of our employees and how we treat our customers is so fundamental to what we do."

To tap into the climate/outlook toward teaching and training in your organization, ask yourself the following questions:

- Do people in the organization perceive it is in their best interest to share their knowledge and to cooperate, rather than compete?
- Do people know how proposed new ideas will benefit them?
- Does the system of rewards, advancement, and recognition support those working for continuous improvement?
- Are education and training available to everyone?

Bill Kent, owner and CEO of Horner Equipment of Florida had built a $50 million company by having all employees involved in their own training. Employees teach each other subjects ranging from customer satisfaction to export to distribution. Groups meet after hours for 60 minutes every other week for 12 weeks. Kent is convinced that if he spends 5% of his salary base to bring new ideas to employees, "the benefits will be tremendous both for the people and the business."

77. Learn from Mistakes

Too often we think of mistakes only as costly failures. Actually, they can be very helpful if we learn from them. Example: Fred DeLuca needed money to cover his college tuition. He was 17, working at a minimum-wage job, and his family had limited means. Without financial help, there was no way he could afford to go to college.

DeLuca approached a friend who might loan him some money. Instead, he was offered a suggestion: Why not rent a small site and open a sandwich shop? The overhead would be low, the work relatively simple.

DeLuca and his friend tested the market by looking over the competition – their menus and their marketing strategies. Then DeLuca opened his first store, for a low $165 a month rent. *This was his big mistake.* The site was in a low-traffic location.

A quick learner – DeLuca opened a second store in a high-profile, high-traffic area. It was an immediate success, and within a few months, he opened a third. Barely five years later, he had a thriving chain of 10 stores.

The next step was to franchise his idea. Within eight years, the company had 300 outlets. Today, Subway Restaurants has nearly 17,000 stores in 74 countries throughout the world.

78. Consider Other Options

The problem is never how to get new, innovative thoughts into your mind, but how to get old ones out.

—Dee Hock, founder of Visa

Sometimes it's not *what* you know *now*. Sometimes it's not *who* you know *now*. Sometimes it's nothing more than the willingness to work hard and be creative that keeps us on the pathway to success.

Barbara Kavovit had gone to college and had earned a degree in finance. Although she knew nothing about home repair, she thought she saw a niche she could fill – a way "to go where no woman had gone before."

Her first step was to greet people in a supermarket parking lot, hand them a business card, and say: "I'm starting a home improvement company and would like to help you."

Kavovit began to get calls asking her to clean gutters, fix cracked tiles, seal driveways, and adjust doorknobs. She accepted every job . . . and hired a handyman to help her. She learned all that she could on the job, and began to take classes in home construction.

After six months, she sent a note to a contact at IBM saying she had a small crew who could handle improvements in their corporate headquarters." It was followed for three months by telephone calls and, finally, a series of personal meetings. The result: a two-year contract to do all of the small repairs in IBM's corporate headquarters during the evening and weekend hours.

Within a few years, Kavovit found herself the founder, president and CEO of Anchor Construction Inc., one of the 50 most profitable construction companies in New York City. She has also formed Barbara K Enterprises, which plans to market a user-friendly toolbox, accompanied by a how-to booklet that explains how to complete 20 different home repair projects.

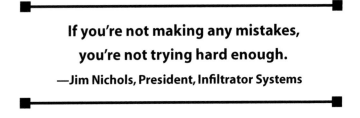

**If you're not making any mistakes,
you're not trying hard enough.**
—Jim Nichols, President, Infiltrator Systems

79. Don't Hide Your Talents

Hidden talents can't be used. You bring out your best by deliberately capitalizing on them every day. The first step is to be sure people know that you are interested in them. Try this little checklist. I call it *The Friendliness Quiz*:

1. Do you greet people as soon as you
   see them?   ☐Yes ☐No
2. Do you call people by name?   ☐Yes ☐No
3. Are you a friendly and helpful person?   ☐Yes ☐No
4. Do you give the impression that
   you enjoy life?   ☐Yes ☐No
5. Do you feel you have a good
   sense of humor?   ☐Yes ☐No
6. Are you generous with praise?   ☐Yes ☐No
7. Do you look for the good rather than
   the bad in people?   ☐Yes ☐No
8. Do you reflect optimism rather than
   pessimism when facing problems?   ☐Yes ☐No
9. Are you considerate about others'
   feelings?   ☐Yes ☐No
10. Do you try to be positive rather than
    negative when expressing yourself?   ☐Yes ☐No
11. Do you avoid criticizing people if
    possible?   ☐Yes ☐No
12. Are you patient with people?   ☐Yes ☐No

Total Number of YES Answers _____

How did you do on the quiz? Count the number of your **YES** answers. A score of 10 or higher marks you as perceptive and knowledgeable in your relationships. An average score is 8. A score of 6 or lower strongly suggests that you focus on improving in those areas.

80. Measure Your Own Effectiveness

You may own (or control) all of the assets. You may be personally liable for all of the debts. You may be the only one who can sign checks or contracts. But if you are to grow as a leader, you must get exceptional performance from other people as well as yourself. You also will have to learn how to lead people who have talents and abilities greater than your own.

Success as a leader requires concentration on:

- **Mistake/risk tolerance:** How do you react when things go wrong? If you always look for someone to blame, you'll always find them. Remember though, people afraid of being blamed will seldom take a risk. If that's what you want, that's what you'll get ... but don't be surprised if those people don't accomplish much. Look for *what's* wrong before asking *who's* wrong. Be a problem-solver, not a people-blamer.
- **Persistence:** Success and failure have the same root: a desire to achieve. Don't blame people for trying. Be glad that they did.
- **Willpower:** Brainpower without willpower is *no* power. How do you develop willpower? By assigning yourself difficult goals over an extended period of time and systematically working to achieve them. You must be sure you know the difference between activities, which are a means to an end, and results, which are the desired outcome. You also must know the difference between efficiency (doing things right) and effectiveness (doing the right things right).

- **Accountability:** To avoid failure, you must accomplish something. Avoiding failure is not the same as achieving success. Being security-oriented can be a great hindrance. In the process of trying to make things easier and more secure, you are in fact weakening yourself. Don't apologize for giving difficult jobs to people, you are doing them a favor.

- **Planning:** Always ask, "*Who* will do *what* by *when*?" The most valuable people are the ones who have learned to be accountable. When you do not determine accountability, you favor those you need least and turn off those you need most. Thinking is the hardest work there is. Don't avoid it. Most of the time, we are too preoccupied with *doing* to take the time to *think*. Too seldom these days do we hear someone say, "I don't know. I need to think about it."

- **Service:** The essence of customer satisfaction can be found in the question, "How can I serve you?" Too often, we ignore customers and give them the definite impression that our business exists solely for our own benefit.

- **Confidence building:** Confidence grows with achievement. We must know our strengths and learn to capitalize on them at work. When weakness prevails, we can never bring out our best. The Japanese have been comparatively disadvantaged in terms of access to major markets, low soil productivity, population density, and limited natural resources ... but they have become one of the most competitive nations in the world's markets. Why? Because Japanese employers first ask: "What can this person do well and how can the company benefit from these strengths?"

Unfortunately, too many American employers still concentrate on penalizing employees for what they can't do.

- **Self-motivation:** The greatest motivator of people is not money, but genuine benefit. Irresistible is the offer whose demonstrated benefit far outweighs its expense. If I tell you: "You can't beat my price," you will challenge me. But if the advantages of what I offer are clearly superior, you will find a way to acquire it. You can't motivate other people. But you can create an environment in which they will be self-motivated.

- **"We" vs. "They":** In my consulting work, I have devised a simple way to assess the climate for cooperation in an organization. I count the number of times I hear supervisors and managers use the word "they" instead of "we." If it's "they" most of the time, it tells me that these are people who do not consider themselves a part of the team. There is limited involvement and minimal commitment.

- **Performance:** Competence without accomplishment is worthless. Intentions have no value without results. People need to know what is expected of them and how they're doing. They need guidance. They need to be paid and promoted according to their performance. Most of all, they need the opportunity to *bring out their best!*

9

Attitude Makes the Difference

You are never a loser until you quit trying.

—Mike Ditka, Football Coach

---

81. Use Fear to Help You

Even the most successful people get nervous before trying something new. When that happens, though, they forget their short-term discomfort and look to the long-term results.

They can do this because they have learned to:

- **Recognize what fear can do.** Fear brings on mediocrity, dulls creativity, and sets a person up to lose. Feed your faith, not your fear. Deliberately test yourself in situations where you must overcome fear.

- **Skip the excuses.**

Ninety-nine percent of failures come from people who have the habit of making excuses.
—George Washington Carver

Carver was born into slavery and grew up in the south during an age of extreme prejudice. He earned a master's degree in agricultural chemistry and was head of the agricultural department at Tuskegee Institute in Alabama, where he became one of the leading botanists of his time. He could have made excuses; instead he made history.

- **Pay the price.** Growth requires discipline. Discipline is gained by facing change, taking risks and overcoming fear.

There has not been a person in our history who led a life of ease whose name is worth remembering.
—Theodore Roosevelt

82. Look for Good News

You don't concentrate on risks. You concentrate on results.

—Charles Yeager, test pilot

While still in his mid-teens, Alfred Nobel began working in his father's company, which made war weapons, pipes and steam engines. But after the Crimean War ended in 1856, orders declined and the firm soon went bankrupt.

Young Alfred was fascinated by a product his chemistry tutor had shown him – nitroglycerine. Unstable, explosive, and very dangerous, it was used only sparingly.

Nobel worked relentlessly to modify the liquid so it could be used in construction. His solution: dynamite. Orders poured in, and his invention became widely used to help build roads, tunnels, and canals throughout the world. Before his death, he held more than 350 patents, but dynamite remains the one for which he is best remembered.

A peaceful man, Nobel was disheartened when dynamite became used as an instrument of war. When he died, he left his fortune to the Nobel Foundation, sponsor of the annual Nobel Prizes for Peace, Literature, Chemistry, Physics, Economic Science, and Physiology/Medicine.

83. Carefully Select a New Job

Accepting the wrong job is a triple loss, 1) it's bad for employers because expectations will not be met, 2) it's bad for those hired because they won't last and 3) it's bad for the job because it won't get done properly. The decision justifies extensive, thorough up-front investigation in order to make the best choices. Here are a few suggestions that will help:

To get the most out of each interview:

1. Prepare yourself fully.
2. Decide on questions you need to have answered in advance.
3. Use notes, but only to assist your memory
4. Concentrate on questions pertaining to what the employer expects.
5. Listen for evidence of objectivity (vs. subjectivity) in assessing progress.
6. Look for evidence of how performance is measured.
7. Focus on learning as much as possible.

Be ready to answer these questions:
- **Why did you leave your last job?**
- **What did you like best about your last job?**
- **What was your most interesting job or project?**
- **What do you see yourself doing five years from now?**

After the interview, your decision can be based on these questions:

- Do you meet all the job requirements?
- Do you have the mental and/or physical capabilities necessary to do the work?
- Do you have the knowledge and skills essential to success?
- Does the position fit with your longer range plan?

84. Stay Positive

Let life be a sunrise, not a metronome.

Only positive people can consistently bring out their best. Staying optimistic should be easy in our country. Just think of what we have:

- Almost unlimited natural resources.
- Food so plentiful over-eating has become a major problem.
- Churches of our choice.
- 100 million jobs.
- Freedom to go anywhere you want, with the transportation to get there.
- A judicial system that is the envy of the rest of the world.
- Social Security.

- Medicare.
- Unemployment insurance.
- Public schools and plentiful scholarships.

Given all of these advantages, there is an unlimited opportunity to make ourselves what we want to be.

85. Demonstrate Accountability

We show our definition of accountability every day in simple, obvious ways by:

- Arriving on time.
- Limiting the personal use of company property.
- Leaving personal matters at home.
- Respecting others' space.
- Respecting confidentiality.
- Avoiding destructive gossip.
- Communicating areas of concern before they become major problems.
- Taking the initiative to solve problems.

Only when our daily actions reveal we *are* accountable can we expect that even our best intentions will be believed.

86. Build Your Own Confidence

**Confidence turns on the lights.
Overconfidence turns them off.**

Some people acquire or learn a sense of "helplessness." It starts with the conviction that nothing can be done, and whatever they attempt probably won't work.

The main barriers they face aren't *outside* their control, but *inside* their own minds. Curing a lack of confidence is absolutely essential to bringing out your best.

Louis L'Amour, whom many believe was America's best Western novelist, prepared himself to write about real people by doing any job he could find. He left his hometown of Jamestown, South Dakota at age 15 and found himself herding cattle, bailing water out of ships bound for Asia, mixing concrete and digging ditches. His objective was to someday make use of every experience in one of his stories. It worked. L'Amour is the only novelist in history to receive both the Presidential Medal of Freedom and the Congressional Gold Medal. He published 90 novels and 23 short story collections. There are more than 260 million copies of his books in print.

Duke Kahanamoku is usually credited with being the Father of Surfing. The Hawaiian became famous when he won an Olympic Gold medal as a swimmer but found his greatest challenge in surfing. One day, friends were amazed when he calmly walked from a beach toward monstrous waves and walls of water some over 50 feet high. He didn't think about falling but rode a huge wave 1½ miles, farther than any surfer had gone before.

87. Seek Responsibility

A society stays free only when most of its people seek responsibility. It is the requirement that makes laws work. It is the indispensable element of personal satisfaction and organizational effectiveness.

Responsibility means doing the right thing whenever you can:

- Even when you are not feeling your best.
- Even when no one else will know about it.
- Even when the recipient does not seem totally deserving.
- Even when there is no direct benefit to yourself.
- Even when the recipient is not appreciative.
- Even when conditions aren't completely right.
- Even when you are criticized because the support is too small to be helpful.
- Even when there is no praise for what you did.

Responsible people never count on luck or chance. They make things happen and find there is no substitute for the satisfaction they feel.

Tyrone "Muggsy" Bogues at 5'3" is the shortest player in the history of the National Basketball Association. But his greatest accomplishment is taking responsibility for his future by using height to his advantage. Darting among the players one and two feet taller, he became the NBA's all-time leader in assists-to-turnover rates. He has never thought of himself as disadvantaged because he's always thinking about "making the next step."

88. Get On With It

Failure is a vital part of life. In fact, it's necessary. The challenge is, how long will it take to get up and get going.

You didn't walk before you crawled.

You fell many times before you took steps.

You inhaled a lot of water before you could float or swim.

You took a lot of tests before you graduated.

In any contest, there is a winner . . . and a loser.

Keep in mind:

- Michael Jordan was dropped from the team in high school.
- Bill Gates dropped out of college.
- Babe Ruth held the strikeout record as well as the home run record.
- Sam Walton almost filed for bankruptcy before WalMart survived.
- Before he sold his first car and saved his company from ruin, Henry Ford had only $223.65 to his name.

If you worry about failing, you may not try. If you don't try, you will never succeed. Trying is the beginning of everything. When you don't try, defeat is your only destiny.

89. Avoid Handicapping Yourself

You've just suffered a serious reversal. You're angry and discouraged. Yet, as bad as things are, you have a great opportunity to learn from the experience ... to use it to create an advantage for the next time.

Rich Gannon, quarterback of the Oakland Raiders, is meticulous in creating an advantage for himself and his team. He arrives for practice early and leaves late. On Tuesday, the team's day off, he studies film for hours. After memorizing scores of his opponents' formations, his wife quizzes him on them two nights a week. She marks every mistake and makes him give the correct answer until he gets them all right. Bottom line: Gannon set a record in the 2002 season by having 10 games passing for more than 300 yards, and was selected as the most valuable player in the National Football League.

It's hard for many people to be honest about having failed, but failure is an inevitable part of living and working. And it's not necessarily all bad. Bill Rosenberg sold watermelons in front of his father's Boston grocery store and never stopped selling.

He quit school in the 8th grade but listened carefully when his father told him that his reputation was worth more than money. He applied that knowledge years later in his donut shop when he told customers that if they didn't like his coffee it was free. Rosenberg's Dunkin' Donuts, Inc. became the world's best-known chain of its type with 5,000 stores in 40 countries. He also founded the International Franchise Association. Franchising now accounts for about 42% of retail sales in the U.S. and employs 8 million people.

Are you self-handicapped? Look for these clues:

- procrastination
- self-pity
- excuses
- blaming
- refusal to try

90. Disarm Opponents

Smart people know what to look for.
Wise people know what to overlook.

Too often we forget that modesty and humility can get better results than power or force.

Ulysses G. Grant was a most extraordinary leader. Dedicated and tenacious . . . he was also extremely humble regarding his many achievements.

Born in 1822, Grant graduated from West Point at the age of 21. He was named commander of U.S. forces at age 42, at the same time becoming the country's first lieutenant general since George Washington. Within a year, he accepted the surrender of Lee's Confederate Army, essentially ending the Civil War. Three years later, he became the country's first four-star general. In 1868, he was elected President of the United States, an office he held for two terms.

Of Grant, General William T. Sherman said: "He fixes in his mind what is the true objective and abandons all minor ones. If his plan goes wrong, he is never discon-certed, but promptly devises a new one, and is sure to win in the end."

A Confederate general, James Longstreet, a close friend of Grant's before the war, added: "(Grant) will fight us every hour of the day until the end of this war." And so he did.

Grant stayed modest and humble, even as his fame and reputation grew. He made it a point to praise his subordinates and give them credit for what was achieved. He expected them to be specific with their facts when presenting plans and did the same in return. He was clear and concise verbally and with written orders, and he made certain his commanders "knew exactly what he wanted, why and when he wanted it."

Grant treated his men with courtesy and respect. He would not tolerate gossip or back-biting. He never swore. He tried to command by encouragement, never embar-rassment.

We bring out our best when opponents expect us to take the easy way, the path of least resistance. We disarm them when what we show is way beyond their expectations.

IT'S NOT EASY

To Apologize
To Begin Over
To Admit Error
To Keep Trying
To Take Advice
To Be Unselfish
To Be Charitable
To Face a Sneer
To Avoid Mistakes
To Be Considerate
To Endure Success
To Profit by Mistakes
To Keep Out Of a Rut
To Forgive and Forget
To Think and Then Act
To Make the Best of Little
To Subdue an Unruly Temper
To Recognize the Silver Lining
To Shoulder a Deserved Blame

BUT IT ALWAYS PAYS

10

Define Success

91. Sharpen Your Competitive Edge

To be successful you must be in demand. To be in demand, you must sharpen your competitive edge. This requires concentration on five bedrock principles. None are complicated, but each can be deceptively difficult to accomplish.

1. **Understand that avoiding failure is not the same as achieving success.** If you have good intentions but never see them through, they are worthless.
2. **Take advantage of your strengths and minimize the impact of your weaknesses.** It is always important not to trust your instincts exclusively without counsel. Successful people are aware that they are not "islands." They appreciate the people behind the scenes who had a lot to do with helping them.
3. **Realize that the most important ability is accountability.** Accountability precedes improvement. For competitors, the never-ending quest at all times and

in all places is to answer the question: "What do we mean by performance?" Performance requires accountable people who always determine *who* will do *what* by *when*.

4. **Accept the reality that time is not on your side.** Change will come more quickly than you think. As the saying goes: "All things come to those who wait" – but they get only what's left by those who have hustled!

5. **Change before you have to.** When you get to the bottom line, life is anticipation, and death is no change. Anticipation is the least understood key to personal vitality. Planners create. Change-resisters vegetate. Planning is creating a future for your organization. If you don't plan, your future is in someone else's hands.

To be sure your competitive edge is as sharp as it can be, ask yourself:

- What am I doing that is no longer serving its purpose? Do I know? Do I have evidence?
- What am I doing that is not cost-effective or consistent with my priorities?
- What am I doing that may be restricting my growth, limiting my future, dulling my competitive edge?

Above all, keep this in mind every day: Your competitive edge is *you*! If you want to be competitive, don't wait another day – get on with it!

92. Keep Goals in Focus

It's so easy to get sidetracked by the daily grind, we tend to lose sight of our goals.

Jack Canfield and Mark Victor Hansen, authors of the *Chicken Soup for the Soul* series helped themselves stay focused by cutting out *The New York Times* best-seller-list, putting the title of their first book in the Number One position, and posting it where they would see it every day. They used the modified best-seller list to remind them of the steps they needed to take to achieve their goal.

Canfield and Hansen had people write letters of commitment to buy the book when it came out, and showed them to publishers to prove that the title would sell. They put a notice in their newsletter asking readers to time their purchases so the book would hit *The New York Times* best-seller list. Eventually, the book actually *did* reach the top of the list.

After the stock market crash in 1929, hotel magnate Conrad Hilton hit rock bottom. People weren't traveling. His creditors were threatening to foreclose. He actually borrowed money from a bellboy so he could eat.

Hilton came upon a photograph of New York's Waldorf-Astoria Hotel with six kitchens, 200 cooks, 500 waiters, 2,000 rooms and its own private hospital. He cut it out and wrote across the front: "The Greatest of Them All." He put the picture in his wallet, and when he had a desk again, he slipped it under the glass top. From then on, it was always in front of him. Eighteen years later, in October 1949, Conrad Hilton acquired the Waldorf-Astoria. The photograph had helped him maintain his focus.

Actor Jim Carrey is one of the highest-paid movie stars in the world . . . but it wasn't always that way. As he worked his way up, he put in many years of hard work and had lots of setbacks.

At one point, Carrey wrote himself a check for $10 million and postdated it several years into the future. He added the notation: "For Services Rendered." The check represented the amount he planned to earn *per movie* once he became a big star. Everywhere he went, he carried the check in his back pocket.

When the date Carrey had written on the check arrived, he was in fact earning $10 million per picture. His determination – his focus – made the difference.

93. Puncture Pressure Points

**We can be happy with little
and miserable with much.**

—William Dempster Hoard, publisher and agriculturalist

Pressure comes with success. There's no getting around it. But you don't have to let it dominate your life. Elvis Presley was fabulously wealthy and admired by millions when he destroyed his life with drugs and died young. On the other hand, Mother Teresa donated her life to countless thousands of helpless, hopeless people. Without her, they would have died young. She was so absorbed in her work she didn't think it was stressful and lived a long time.

While there are no guaranteed techniques for puncturing pressure points, there are a number of guidelines you can use:

- **Vent your problem to a confidant.** Select someone you can trust – not just a great listener, but someone who will keep what you say in confidence.
- **Focus on the positive outcome.** Convince yourself that you can use pressures you feel to help you grow. Think: "Now I realize that I must never get myself into this kind of situation again."
- **Don't wait too long.** If the pressure is strong enough to bother you, do something about it. Waiting isn't going to make the situation any better, and it could make it worse.
- **Take charge.** Put yourself in a position to either divert or stop the pressure. If you have to make an important presentation, take the time to prepare for it. If you have something to get off your chest, do it and don't procrastinate.
- **Congratulate yourself.** Once you've been confronted with a pressure situation and have been able to successfully face it down, *take credit for it*. Not only has your skill brought the situation under control, but you can now feel more confident about the future.

94. Create an Inside Advantage

All too often, we tend to blame outside influences for our setbacks and failures. The problem, we contend, is: an unfair competitor ... an unexpected change in the marketplace . . . technology which caught us by surprise . . . a regulatory agency . . . or an unexpected lawsuit.

Any of those things may occur, of course, but most problems result not from external causes but a failure to capitalize on our own personal "inside" advantages. We provide these advantages for ourselves every day in basic ways when we:

1. Show up on time.
2. Listen.
3. Never hide the truth.
4. Don't look back.
5. Avoid unhealthy choices.
6. Become accountable.
7. Don't make excuses.
8. Deliver what is promised.
9. Don't try to be perfect.
10. Change before a crisis.

Our inside advantage is created not only by ourselves but those we involve on our team. It can be lost quickly when we are not careful about who we hire.

Surveys have indicated why people are or are not hired for key positions. The following results are very revealing:

Reasons for Hiring
- Most "know-how"
- Best track record
- Best "chemistry" with selectors
- Best people-handler
- Most highly motivated

- Best growth potential
- Best references and reputation
- Most enthusiasm for the job
- Most imaginative and innovative
- Available at a lower salary
- Available now or before other applicants

Notice that the first two reasons can both be documented quite easily, whereas the "best chemistry" factor deals with personality and behavior factors – things that historically have been difficult to pin down or be objective about.

Reasons for Not Hiring
- Too many job changes
- Reluctance to relocate
- Bad "chemistry" with boss(es)
- Unrealistic salary demands
- Lack of needed skills
- Poor employment record.
- Poor interview (unprepared, uninterested, unresponsive)
- Little growth potential
- Personality problems revealed in reference checks
- Long periods of unemployment

Consider how some of those reasons are linked. The first two are obviously related and can be quickly and easily handled. But again, the issue of "bad chemistry" with the boss(es) rears its ugly head. How can you deal with it? First, try to uncover objective information on which to base a decision. This will give you *a 'people' advantage.*

The key is to help individuals achieve their personal goals as company goals are met.

95. Don't Feed Failure

A failure will teach you a hundred times more than a success.

—Bill Coleman, BEA Systems, Inc.

For over 35 years, I have been studying the reasons why so many people in leadership positions do not succeed. I have concluded there are two root causes:

- **They have not learned effective ways to:**

  1. Set clear, measurable objectives.
  2. Get other people involved in their work-planning and problem-solving.
  3. Integrate their work with the others who depend on them.
  4. Be accountable versus blaming others.

- **They do not understand the importance of self-discipline and have not taught themselves how to:**

  1. Be consistent and predictable in their behavior.
  2. Avoid "cronyism" in hiring, making assignments, or promoting people.

3. Anticipate how they must change and adapt to new people, job content, and circumstances.
4. Determine which people are "stretchable" and which are not.
5. Avoid power plays and making themselves look good at the expense of others.

The primary responsibility of leaders is to be sure they know who the best performers are and why. The best performers have learned how to:

- Get the best results.
- Select promotable people.
- Train and develop new leaders.
- Encourage new ways of doing things.
- Support creativity.
- Accept constructive criticism.
- Define performance and reward it.
- Build strong teams.
- Deal promptly with mismatched people and jobs.

What does leadership require? You should:

- Be visible and accessible.
- Insist on direct contact and negotiation, as opposed to depending upon edicts, emails or memos.
- Create well-informed teams at all levels.
- Concentrate on problem prevention by means of open analysis and input from the bottom up.
- Find many ways to praise and acknowledge the "behind-the-scenes" people who are often taken for granted.

- Weed out those who aren't carrying their load. To keep marginal contributors is to deny your dependence on the best people, and you simply cannot afford to live that kind of lie.
- Showcase those who build strong and effective teams.
- Engage outside help to supplement and complement your strengths.

96. Acknowledge Mistakes

Too often, we lose our best people because of our own mistakes. We frequently:

1. Do not make policies and procedures clear.
2. Do not differentiate between major and minor mistakes.
3. Do not get pertinent facts but act on rumors and unjustified opinions.
4. Delay too long in taking action.
5. Intimidate sensitive people by losing emotional control.
6. Assume too much about your training needs.
7. Do not listen to learn *why* certain actions were taken.
8. Limit inputs to only a few "favorite" people.
9. Fail to document what actually happened and the steps taken for improvement.
10. "Brand" some people for past mistakes and make them feel like they can never regain favor.

You are likely to have many more "inside advantages" than you think ... especially if you learn how to retain the best people.

97. Exceed Expectations

Difficulty is what we allow it to be.

Don't stay with a plan that isn't working. Try another route. The results may be better than you think. Example:

In college, Paul Hornung was outstanding. At Notre Dame in 1956, he led the team in rushing, passing, scoring, kickoff returns, punting, punt returns, and passes broken up. That year, Notre Dame had a record of two wins and eight losses ... but Paul Hornung won the Heisman Trophy as college football's finest player. He remains the only player to win the Heisman while playing for a losing team.

Hornung was drafted by the Green Bay Packers, and in 1957 and 1958, played quarterback, halfback, and fullback ... but his statistics were mediocre and he became discouraged. He even thought of retiring.

In 1959, a new coach arrived – Vince Lombardi.

Lombardi wanted Hornung to be his starting halfback, and gave him an ultimatum: "Your quarterback days are over. You're either going to be my left halfback or you're not going to make it in pro football."

Instead of feeling insulted, Hornung took Lombardi's comments as a challenge. He felt an added incentive to excel in football and vowed to do whatever it took to make that happen.

Hornung could run, pass, kick, catch, block and tackle. Over a span of nine seasons with Green Bay, he rushed for 3,711 yards, had 1,480 yards in receptions, kicked for 338 points, and passed for 383 yards and five touchdowns. He scored 62 touchdowns, kicked 190 conversions, and booted 66 field goals for a total of 760 points. In 1959, 1960 and 1961, he was the National Football League's scoring leader. In 1960 and 1961, he was the NFL's Most Valuable Player. In 1961, he set an NFL record with 176 points. He entered the College Football Hall of Fame in 1985, and in 1986, was inducted into the Pro Football Hall of Fame.

Hornung gave the Green Bay Packers leadership and poise. He inspired his teammates to play better.

Vince Lombardi called him "the most versatile man who ever played the game."

98. Open Up

Power based on reason lasts longer than either popularity or promises.

Effective communication involves the ability to convey a complete message as well as read or hear a message and avoid misinterpretation. Good communicators learn to express thoughts clearly, accurately, completely, and concisely, to listen attentively, and to ask pertinent questions.

For example:

- **Poor communication:** "We must notify the Berkeley Company that we are raising our prices."

- **Better:** "Joe Smith will notify the Berkeley Company on July 6 (*setting a date*) that our prices are being raised by 10 percent (*specifying the amount*) to offset the increasing cost of copper (*stating the reason*)."

Open communication involves not just facts but the flow of ideas, information, feelings and perceptions. Face-to-face conversations are better because they provide for an interpretation of body language as well as words.

Open communication is vital in these areas:

- Good news – Recognition of individual or group accomplishment, new developments in products or service, the attainment of goals.
- Bad news – Missed objectives, increases in cost, slippage in sales or profits, lost customers, missed opportunities, poor quality control, or other disappointing conditions. It's better for people to hear it directly than from someone else.
- Plans – What is proposed for the future, both short-term and long-term.
- Policies – Guides to action, rules of conduct, strategies for the growth and development and basic commitments to certain relationships, actions and responsibilities.
- Changes – The modification of assignments, schedules, priorities, dates, standards, and procedures.
- What is expected.
- How we are doing.
- Ways to improve.
- Answers to questions, suggestions, and complaints.

99. Find Ways to Serve

The key to fulfillment lies in how close we come to achieving our potential. How honest can we be with ourselves in response to the question *Am I Doing All I Can?* Are you sure? Do you:

1. Gain all you can ...

   without hurting others?

2. Save all you can ...

   without hurting yourself?

3. Praise all you can ...

   without nurturing vanity?

4. Serve all you can ...

   who can't help themselves?

5. Give all you can ...

   of your surplus energy?

6. Renounce all you can ...

   that is harmful?

7. Reach all you can ...

   with your personal example?

8. Teach all you can ...

   who need your knowledge?

9. Console all you can ...

   who are sick in mind or body?

10. Support all you can ...

   causes you want to outlive you?

100. Make Yourself Needed

The ultimate compliment is, "The worse the situation, the better s/he gets."

When Thomas J. Stanley, then a professor at Georgia State University, began to study how people become millionaires, he learned some interesting facts:

- Wealth is not the same as income.
- It's not luck, inheritance, or even intelligence that builds fortunes.
- Most fortunes are built by hard work, perseverance, self-discipline and saving.

The average person with a net worth of one million dollars or more is usually a person who has lived their adult life in the same town; owns a small business, has been married once . . . is still married, and lives in a middle-class neighborhood. How did they do it?

- **They live below their means.**
- **They work on specific goals.**
- **They don't stay with things that don't work.**
- **They cultivate good advice.**
- **They make themselves needed.**

Whatever your career preference, the key is to keep yourself and your skills in demand. Your competitive edge is you. Your highest priority investment by far, is to focus on the actions which will *bring out your best*.

INDEX

Additional Information

For more information about Dr. Roger Fritz's consulting and presentation topics or for a catalog of books, audio tapes, CD-ROMS, reprints, software and other products, contact:

> Organization Development Consultants
> Phone: 630.420.7673
> Fax: 630.420.7835
> Email: RFritz3800@aol.com
> Website: http://www.rogerfritz.com